SQL
QuickStart Guide™

SQL

QuickStart Guide™

The Simplified Beginner's Guide to Managing,
Analyzing, and Manipulating Data with SQL

Walter Shields

Editor: Marilyn Burkley
Cover Illustration and Design: Katie Poorman, Copyright © 2019 by ClydeBank Media LLC
Interior Design: Katie Poorman, Copyright © 2019 by ClydeBank Media LLC

First Edition (edited) | Last Updated: 3/2/2020

ISBN-13: 9781945051753 (paperback) | 9781945051234 (hardcover) | 9781945051838 (eBook)

Library of Congress Control Number: 2019950712

Author ISNI: 0000 0004 6515 9557

Ordering Information: Please visit www.clydebankmedia.com/orders or call (888) 386-2624. Special discounts are available on quantity purchases by corporations, associations, and others.

Publisher's Cataloging-In-Publication Data
(Prepared by The Donohue Group, Inc.)

Names: Shields, Walter, 1975- author.
Title: SQL quickstart guide : the simplified beginner's guide to managing, analyzing, and manipulating data With SQL / Walter Shields.
Other Titles: SQL quick start guide
Description: First Edition (edited). | [Albany, New York] : ClydeBank Technology, [2019] | Includes bibliographical references and index.
Identifiers: ISBN 9781945051234 (hardcover) | ISBN 9781945051753 (paperback) | ISBN 9781945051838 (ebook)
Subjects: LCSH: SQL (Computer program language)--Handbooks, manuals, etc. | Database management--Computer programs--Handbooks, manuals, etc. | Computer programming--Vocational guidance. | Querying (Computer science)--Vocational guidance. | LCGFT: Handbooks and manuals.
Classification: LCC QA76.73.S67 S55 2019 (print) | LCC QA76.73.S67 (ebook) | DDC 005.756--dc23

I would like to give a special thanks to my family Julien, Max, Elke, and Norma. I couldn't have written this book without their patience and support.

Contents

PART I – CREATING YOUR SQL LEARNING ENVIRONMENT

PART II – WRITING SQL STATEMENTS

PART III – MORE ADVANCED SQL TOPICS

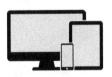

BEFORE YOU START READING, DOWNLOAD YOUR FREE DIGITAL ASSETS!

 Free Audiobook Version of This Book*

 Sample Database (required for examples)

 SQL Software Download Links & Instructions

 SQL Statement Reference Guide

 Video Tutorial

DOWNLOAD DIGITAL ASSETS NOW:

www.clydebankmedia.com/sql-assets

* Must be a first time Audible user in the United States, United Kingdom, France or Germany.
Audible membership is $14.95/month after the first 30 days. Easily cancel anytime.

Introduction

With each passing day—really with each passing second—greater and greater quantities of data are collected. In the time it takes you to finish this sentence, over 500,000 Google search queries will be submitted.[1] In a single minute, over 300 hours of video content will be uploaded to YouTube.[2] Our capacity to store data continues to grow. Meanwhile, smartphones and social media have turned everyday individuals across the globe into a rapidly (exponentially) growing army of data generators, constantly creating new records that reveal our current interests, activities, thoughts, and feelings. Businesses and government agencies of all kinds are accepting the reality that maximum efficiency and maximum profitability cannot be achieved without harnessing the power of data.

THE PHENOMENAL REALITY OF BIG DATA

fig. 1

GOOGLE

- Processes 40,000 search queries every second.

- Processed 27.5 billion search queries in 2001 compared to 1.2 trillion in 2012 and growing.

YOUTUBE

- 6 hours of video content was uploaded every minute in 2007 compared to 400 hours per minute in 2015 and growing.

FACEBOOK

- Brands and organizations receive a cumulative 34,722 Likes every minute of the day.

- Every month, 30 billion pieces of content are shared.

AMAZON

- Stores data from 152 million customers in 1.4 million servers spread throughout several data centers.

See references 3 and 4 in the back of the book

While the volume of data being generated is astounding in its own right, what is truly mind-boggling is that we have only just begun to make use of it all. Only half of a percent of all data collected is ever analyzed.[5] If individuals, businesses, governments, and other organizations were able to make better use of collected data, then the potential upside would be limitless. Profits and efficiency could be increased, marketers could gain more powerful insight into target audiences, and more fraud and crime could be prevented—and that is just the beginning. The shortfall in data analysis contributes to an incredible demand for skilled data-handling professionals. This is where *you* come in.

You are presumably reading this book because you want to learn SQL (structured query language). You have been perceptive enough to notice the ever-expanding role of data in the world, and you are putting yourself in a position to make the most of it—a very wise decision. Some of you may be studying SQL in a classroom environment, at either the high school or college level. Or perhaps you are a business or government professional looking to develop the skills necessary to carry you forward in your career. Whatever the case may be, this book's straightforward approach to SQL will prove an invaluable resource.

SQL (properly pronounced "ess-cue-ell," though "sequel" is commonly heard) is the translation tool that allows everyday individuals, even those without coding experience, to communicate with a database and turn big data into information they can use to make decisions that affect their business for the better. I have been working with SQL and other forms of big data management for eighteen years, but I can still remember what it was like to be a beginner. It took me a while to warm up to data management. When I first learned how to use Microsoft Access, data management was just another node in the IT field, without the hype that surrounds it in the present day. The quantity of data generated was relatively minuscule in light of today's information overload. Today, every search query made on Google, every post shared on Facebook, and every five-star review in every product category on Amazon is ultimately stored on a server somewhere and is subject to being queried. SQL is the principal analytical tool used to decipher big data, hence the extraordinary demand for individuals trained in the language. The language of data is a language that every modern tech-oriented company speaks to some degree. This book will get you fluent in the language of data.

My Story

My personal road to mastery of SQL began in the late nineties. At the time, opportunities to learn SQL in a formal, institutional setting were quite scarce, as the phenomenon of big data had not come to maturity. In lieu of any real scholastic alternative, I matriculated into the school of hard knocks—I learned SQL by trial and error, mostly error. Even after acquiring a bachelor's degree in computer science and a master's in management information systems, I did not feel that a formal, academic, and sometimes overly theoretical approach to learning was the best pathway to success in the field of data science—a belief I would confirm after working for over eighteen years in a variety of roles using SQL (as well as other programming languages) to manage data systems across several sectors, from startups to Fortune 500 companies, from law to healthcare to big box retail.

If I have learned anything from both my academic and professional wanderings, it is this: there is a much more practical approach to becoming an invaluable resource in your existing or new career in the world of big data. It does not have to be as difficult for you as it was for me. In fact, it was my desire to distill all the lessons I have learned into a simple, practical, hands-on approach to SQL that led me to write this book.

The enthusiasm I have for teaching is actually a product of family values. I was born in Trinidad, a country you have probably heard of but are perhaps unable to place on the map. It is a tiny dual-island country, known formally as "Trinidad and Tobago," located at the northern end of the South American continent and the southern end of the Caribbean Sea. Though the Caribbean may be known for cruises, carnivals, soca, and reggae music, life was not all beaches and coconuts.

My mother was both a literature teacher and a high school principal. When she wasn't at school, she was at home giving piano lessons. She was always sharing ideas, always teaching, and never lacking for students. She considered it a social responsibility to pass her acquired skills and knowledge to others in the community, often working long hours and giving back to those around her in any way she could. The teaching passion extends deep and wide throughout my family tree; I had an aunt, uncle, and grandfather who were all professional educators. Though I have lived in the United States for nearly twenty years, I still return to Trinidad each year to visit family and to reflect on the incredible journey that is life.

When I am not working in the field you can find me in the classroom, where I regularly host SQL and data visualization training courses for beginners and intermediate-level students. I love to code—don't get me wrong—but it is in teaching, in seeing my students succeed, where I find the most joy.

Why I Wrote This Book

My objective in writing this book was to create a definitive beginner's SQL toolbox—the kind of resource I wish I'd had access to when I was just beginning in this field. As I learned from my formal education, a theoretical approach to technical and programming topics is not the most practical, or the most sympathetic to our busy lives and schedules. Other SQL texts spend a lot of time explaining both the history and the computer science theory behind databases and query language. This book aims to take a polite nod toward those topics, covering only what is essential for understanding how a relational database functions, and then blaze on ahead. The rest of the book is designed to equip you, the reader, with a hands-on reusable reference guide to harness big data and turn it into actionable information. The truth of the matter is that learning SQL requires a commitment to regular study and practice. The best teachers do not simply spout information at their students and hope for the best. The best teachers are those who set expectations responsibly and ensure that students adopt a resilient, "can-do" frame of mind. I do not want this book to center around my expertise. Instead, I want it to focus on you and your path to learning. For me it is both a pleasure and a privilege to spend my working hours venturing about in oceans of data. The next challenge lies in helping you comfortably enter these oceans without fear of drowning.

Creating a "QuickStart" resource that can be used by a pure beginner on SQL is an ambitious endeavor. I have worked with hundreds of SQL students, enough to gather a sense of what works and what does not. My passion for teaching SQL has spanned several years and many different professional positions. When you acquire a real proficiency in this skill, you will soon find yourself beset by colleagues looking to you for help. Whether it is an executive who wants targeted data about the latest marketing campaign or a fellow coder who needs your help crafting a query, being handy with SQL has a way of drawing people to you—*if you learn it, they will come.*

My SQL coaching business, SQL Training Wheels, and my data visualization business, Datadecided.com, are truly a culmination and institutionalization of my enthusiasm for teaching the craft. SQL Training Wheels began in a coffee shop in Tribeca, New York, with me and a laptop full of SQL learning materials I had prepared. I had no idea whether anyone was going to show up. I must have underestimated the demand for SQL training, because not only did people show up, *many* people showed up. And they kept coming. Before I knew it, I had a business.

I have discovered over the years, in my capacity as an SQL mentor and coach, that I truly enjoy teaching. Growing up among active academics, I witnessed firsthand the power of imparted knowledge, how it could replenish confidence and promote positive personal transformations. Though New York City is worlds apart from my home in Trinidad, I still recognize and relish that moment when I see a light turn on in a student's mind—their eyes brighten, their anxiety is abated, something clicks! I never get tired of these "lightbulb" moments.

As I continue to improve and expand this training endeavor, working with a rich variety of students with different aptitudes and skill sets, I find myself contemplating the idea of one day expanding my business seaward, back home to the Caribbean. I think it would be a blast teaching a few courses in Trinidad, maybe in Grenada as well. How gratifying it would be to take back the knowledge and experience of my time in the United States while also developing a Caribbean franchise! There is no rule saying you cannot dream big and give back at the same time.

A Word of Encouragement for the Pure Beginner

To be successful in your study of SQL, you must be patient—with the material and especially with yourself. I believe in every student I teach, but my success as a teacher is ultimately measured by that of my students. For the pure beginner, SQL and database management will seem intimidating. Accept it, transcend it; greet the challenge with a tenacious spirit, and you are going to be successful! Here are a few important things to keep in mind for those of you who are brand new to SQL:

» Don't be afraid of making mistakes. There is no shortage of *sandbox* space in this industry. In other words, there are plenty of ways to practice SQL without the potential of "ruining" an existing database, which is a concern for some beginners. A sample database is made available for you to use in conjunction with this book. I want you to take full advantage of it and be open to learning via trial and error.

» Treat this book as a workbook. Highlight, underline, write in the margins. SQL is a topic that is learned by doing, not just reading. I have carefully designed the exercises in this book to reflect real-world scenarios and to slowly build upon each other to fortify what was learned in the previous chapter. If you find a new concept difficult, there is value in going back and working through the fundamentals again.

» Enjoy your study! Do not lose sight of the fact that you are sitting on the cutting edge of information technology, honing a high-demand skill that is poised to radically change the world. It is okay to be a little excited!

The Scope and Focus of This Book

For readers who already possess a basic or even an advanced understanding of SQL, this QuickStart Guide will function as both a refresher and a handy reference text that you can consult when crafting your queries. Also, if you are among the many aspiring SQL coders to have recently enrolled in an SQL course or training program, then this QuickStart Guide will serve as a fantastic primer text and should provide a nice advantage for you in the classroom.

Please note that this book primarily covers the basic SQL toolkit you need to understand and extract useful and actionable information from existing database sources. The standard query methods taught in this text can be done safely without risk of changing the database in any way. However, in one of the later chapters we do briefly cover adding, modifying, and removing entries from a database (known as data manipulation language, or DML). Learning the concepts in the DML chapter is not necessary for extracting information from a database, but it is helpful to know how this process is done, and this chapter may be of some interest to those considering a career in database administration.

SQL and Your Career

SQL is one of the most consistently in-demand coding languages that you can study. It is the gold standard for database administration work, but it is also highly sought after in a host of other technical occupations, including software engineering and development, quality assurance testing, and business analysis, to name a few. In fact, why don't we take a moment and review some of these job descriptions.

» **Database administrator (DBA)**: The database administrator is ultimately responsible for ensuring that the company is using the right tools to store and access their data. DBAs take a leadership role in purchasing or modifying the hardware and software solutions that comprise the company database. Database administrators are also responsible for controlling access to the database. They must set and enforce access permission thresholds, password controls, and so forth.

» **Database developer:** The primary role of the database developer is to continually expand and refine the SQL code used to navigate the database. In many organizations the SQL coders are asked to create preassembled blocks of code that can be easily employed by non-skilled individuals. SQL developers are also often placed in charge of ongoing testing of the database to ensure quality performance and optimized functioning.

» **Data scientist:** Data scientists focus on improving and generating new ways of using data to add value to the business. A data scientist working for Amazon might design a system aimed at using data from your product searches to determine which products you see advertised when you log in to your account.

As our capacity to record and store massive amounts of data continues to expand, so does the differentiation and specialization in the data industry. It is no longer uncommon to find universities offering degrees in database administration, data center operations, and data management. In this rapidly emerging field, SQL is the common tongue, and learning it is your ticket to the big data party.

While the data industry understandably covets SQL-trained individuals, the real-world demand for SQL actually extends even further. In any given industry (not just in big data) you may find a multitude of job positions that utilize SQL. Some of these jobs may not require SQL as a primary skill, but if you are able to bring SQL knowledge to the table while also meeting the rest of the job's requirements, then you will hold a serious advantage over the competition when it comes to getting hired or getting a raise.

If you can develop and demonstrate proficiency in SQL, then you can expect to command a healthy salary in the marketplace. In 2018, the average salary for an SQL-trained worker in the United States was upwards of $80,000.[6] In addition to academic study, you will likely need to acquire some hands-on learning before a company will hire you full time. Many companies offer paid internships that will provide you with the opportunity to put your SQL skills to the test in real-world business environments.

Some of you may be pursuing SQL in an effort to mobilize your career path within the company for which you currently work. Perhaps your acquiring of SQL literacy will clearly create value for your company, and you intend to make a case (or have made a case already) to the powers that be that you should be allotted whatever time and resources are needed to develop this skill. And if you end up becoming a more sought-after commodity in the meantime, well, that is always nice too, right?

The demand for SQL spans a multitude of industries and job types. If a company or industry benefits from storing and analyzing data, then the company and industry are likely to benefit from SQL. Take a moment and try to think of all the businesses out there that could potentially benefit from data analysis. This is not a difficult exercise. It is actually much more challenging to think of businesses that would not benefit; hence the insatiable demand in the marketplace for professionals adept at transcribing big data into business advantages. Full speed ahead!

Chapter by Chapter

There are innumerable ways to learn a new skill. For this particular skill, I've found there is no better way than jumping right in and practicing. This book is designed to get you writing queries as soon as possible. The book is divided into three major parts consisting of three to four chapters each:

» "Part 1: Creating Your SQL Learning Environment" – Part 1 includes an introduction to database terminology and structure, as well as a hands-on section designed to set up the specific database software we will be using in this book. Even if you feel confident that you understand the basics of SQL, we still strongly recommend that you follow along, as this section will explain the specific SQL tools, methods, and strategies we will be using throughout the text.

» "Chapter 1: Understanding Database Structure" – This is the only real "sit down and read" chapter in this book. This chapter introduces the concept of a relational database, the types of data you will encounter, and a brief overview of some of the terminology used. The rest of the text will be definitively hands-on.

» "Chapter 2: SQL Tools and Strategies" – In this chapter, we explain how to get the most out of this book, which is intended to be used in conjunction with free downloadable SQL software (SQLite) and a provided sample SQL database so that you can test out what you have learned immediately after you learn it. This chapter also explains how to make the most of the included self-assessments, guided exercises, and other resources provided in the book.

» "Chapter 3: Exploring a Database in SQLite" – In this chapter, we will open the sample database in an SQL browser and explore its contents. You will familiarize yourself with using an SQL browser to navigate the overall structure of a database, view data on individual database tables, and access the "Execute SQL" tab.

» "Part 2: Writing SQL Statements" – In Part 2, we give you the tools to write simple queries. We start with the basic SELECT statement and then introduce additional SQL keywords that enable us to return more specific results.

» "Chapter 4: Getting Started with Queries" – This chapter introduces the basic SELECT statement, demonstrates how to return data from a specific table using the FROM statement, sort that data alphabetically using ORDER BY, and then limit the results using LIMIT.

» "Chapter 5: Turning Data into Information" – This chapter introduces the WHERE clause and the comparative, logical, and arithmetic operators that it takes as arguments. Chapter 5 also introduces LIKE and the use of wildcards as well as the DATE() function, AND/OR operators, and the CASE statement.

» "Chapter 6: Working with Multiple Tables" – This chapter introduces join statements that allow you to return and compare data from multiple tables using INNER JOIN, LEFT JOIN, and RIGHT JOIN.

» "Chapter 7: Using Functions" – This chapter introduces a powerful collection of calculation tools known as functions, including aggregate, string, and date functions.

» "Part 3: More Advanced SQL Topics" – Part 3 introduces more advanced but very helpful techniques used to enhance the efficiency of writing queries. This part also includes an introduction to data manipulation language (DML), which, unlike all other SQL statements so far, will permanently alter the data in a database.

» "Chapter 8: Subqueries" – This chapter introduces the concept of nesting one query inside of another query, resulting in what is called a subquery. The chapter demonstrates how to use subqueries with a variety of SQL keywords we have already learned, as well as introducing the DISTINCT keyword.

» "Chapter 9: Views" – This chapter introduces virtual tables known as views: queries that are saved and can be executed repeatedly as needed or used as subqueries in other SQL statements.

» "Chapter 10: Data Manipulation Language" – This chapter covers data manipulation language (DML) and introduces the `INSERT`, `UPDATE`, and `DELETE` keywords.

PART I

CREATING YOUR SQL LEARNING ENVIRONMENT

| 1 |
Understanding Database Structure

When learning any new technical skill, you need to know the basic vocabulary to start your journey. We aim to find the right balance: arming you with the fundamental terms and concepts you will need for the remainder of this book, while avoiding unnecessary jargon or advanced concepts. In this chapter, we will introduce the concept of a relational database and showcase the types of data you will encounter in a typical database. We will also introduce the fundamental SQL query: the SELECT statement.

Fundamental Terminology

A "datum" is defined as "a piece of information."[7] **Data** is simply the plural form of datum. Data appears everywhere and is contained in everything, but for practical purposes the term "data" generally refers to recorded or recordable information. One of the simplest tools used to record and visualize data is the *table*. A table is merely a two-dimensional grid consisting of rows and columns.

NOTE

When used in a database, a table may also be referred to as a "base relvar," though in this book we will adhere to the term "table." Please see the Terminology Summary graphic (Figure 5).

This is a table

fig. 2

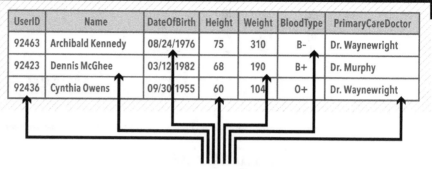

UserID	Name	DateOfBirth	Height	Weight	BloodType	PrimaryCareDoctor
92463	Archibald Kennedy	08/24/1976	75	310	B-	Dr. Waynewright
92423	Dennis McGhee	03/12/1982	68	190	B+	Dr. Murphy
92436	Cynthia Owens	09/30/1955	60	104	O+	Dr. Waynewright

These are data

As you can see in Figure 2, the table contains different types of data. Data can be names, numbers, dates, characters (like "+" or "-"), or it may be presented in a multitude of other formats. Data, in its purest sense, is just information. Therefore, when handling data it behooves us to constrain it appropriately. Look at the table in Figure 2; it appears to store basic information about a group of medical patients. Data about the patients is defined using various formats. There are numbers, names, and dates, and in the BloodType field, a string of two characters is used (a letter and a "+" or "-" character). The formats used to render data are not random. All databases contain something known as ***metadata***, which is data that describes the structure and formatting of the data itself, commonly referred to as "data about the data." For example, the DateOfBirth field may contain metadata that constricts information in the field into mm/dd/yyyy format. The metadata in the Height field might limit data to two digits in length and require that it be expressed in terms of inches.

The term ***database*** can be simply defined as a collection of data arranged for ease and speed of search and retrieval by a computer. The database is often symbolized graphically as a multitiered cylindrical icon (Figure 3) meant to symbolize the stacking of hard disks one on top of another to create a high-capacity data storage center.

Data inside the database is typically stored in a collection of tables. Each table contains a specific set of data, which may relate to and reference other data from other tables within the database.

The patient data table in Figure 2 is just a table, not a database. It could, however, be incorporated into a database alongside other tables, such as those storing information about lab tests, prescription drugs, appointment histories, hospital personnel, doctor information, specialties, and appointment availability.

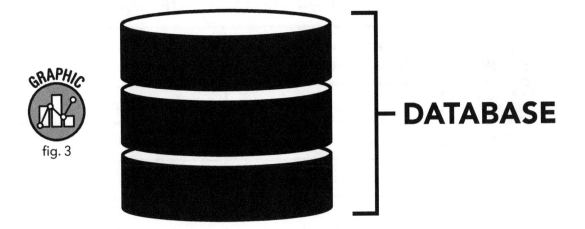

fig. 3 **DATABASE**

The purpose of the database is to facilitate the interaction, organization, and analysis of related data across a multitude of sources. When data is placed in tables that have the capacity to relate to one another within a database, a new level of versatility becomes possible.

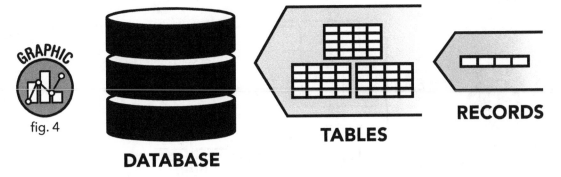

fig. 4 **DATABASE** **TABLES** **RECORDS**

A database is composed of tables, and tables are composed of records.

The *rows* in a given table are considered *records*. They may also be referred to as *tuples*. The **columns** in a table may generally be referred to as *fields*. They may also be called *attributes*. Fields/attributes are the categories used to define the data within the record (row).

NOTE

Throughout this book we will be using the term "records" to describe the rows in a table and "fields" to describe the columns. Please refer to the Terminology Summary in Figure 5.

TERMINOLOGY SUMMARY

fig. 5

Terms we will use throughout this book:	May be referred to elsewhere as:
Record, Row	Tuple
Field, Column	Attribute
Table	Relation, Base Relvar

Every record is broken down into several fields that represent single elements of data describing a specific thing. For example, our table featured in Figure 6 stores information about patients, presumably at a particular hospital or medical practice or in a particular insurance pool. Whatever the nature of the organization, if they keep a database, then that database will likely be composed of several tables. Understanding how tables refer to and relate to one another is key to understanding essential database architecture.

fig. 6

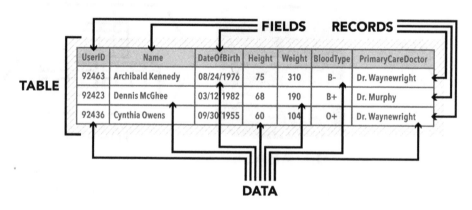

Fundamental Elements of Relational Databases

The *relational database* is a database design that was formally conceived of in 1969 by a computer scientist at IBM named Edgar F. Codd. Codd published an article the following year called "A Relational Model of Data for Large Shared Data Banks."[8] Nine years later, several big players in tech, including IBM and Relational Software Inc. (later to become Oracle), began using relational databases for commercial purposes. Four decades later, the relational model continues to prevail as the most common form of database design.

To gain a rudimentary understanding of how relational databases function, it is important to understand the role of key fields.

PRIMARY KEY FIELD

FOREIGN KEY FIELD

PatientID	PatientName	PrimaryCareDoctorID	PrimaryCareDoctorName	DateOfBirth	Height	Weight	BloodType
92463	Archibald Kennedy	106547	Dr. Waynewright	8/24/1976	75	310	B−
92425	Dennis McGhee	106474	Dr. Murphy	3/12/1982	68	190	B+
92443	Cynthis Owens	106547	Dr. Waynewright	9/30/1955	60	104	O+
92478	William Hampton	106437	Dr. Salazar	6/5/1973	73	175	AB−
92392	Hilda Bass	106783	Dr. Dean	6/10/1997	68	152	B+
92436	Frankie Stone	106437	Dr. Salazar	5/28/1979	68	106	O+
92403	Verna Sullivan	106984	Dr. Conner	7/17/2010	66	125	O+
92398	Merle Doyle	106439	Dr. Frank	1/8/1962	65	143	B−
92442	Ruth Swanson	106954	Dr. Hines	2/15/1970	61	160	O−
92384	Johnathan Singleton	106474	Dr. Murphy	6/2/1970	61	232	AB+
92405	WM Patrick	106439	Dr. Frank	6/11/1955	69	196	O+
92376	Mona Norris	106984	Dr. Conner	10/15/1932	60	98	B+
92399	Rick Gordon	106366	Dr. Hart	1/25/2002	68	149	B+
92408	Don Rivera	106437	Dr. Salazar	7/26/1954	72	185	A−
92389	Sheri Griffin	106211	Dr. Harvey	12/16/1987	78	132	AB−
92466	Guillermo Lawrence	106954	Dr. Hines	2/8/1978	60	219	O+
92310	Felipe Parker	106474	Dr. Murphy	12/10/1998	61	165	O−
92413	Brandi Carlson	106399	Dr. Flowers	11/20/2000	66	112	B+
92398	Floyd Casey	106783	Dr. Dean	12/14/1986	61	203	A−
92439	Patrick Walton	106366	Dr. Hart	8/11/1973	76	189	O+
92421	Vicki Klein	106954	Dr. Hines	11/28/1980	65	98	O+
92381	Cathy Harrison	106474	Dr. Murphy	11/16/1946	78	203	AB−
92393	Ann Guerrero	106783	Dr. Dean	6/25/1974	61	142	B−
92437	Gustavo Bates	106399	Dr. Flowers	2/25/2001	78	165	A−

GRAPHIC

fig. 7

A relational database will contain a multitude of tables similar to the *patient_info* table shown in Figure 7. These tables relate to one another on the basis of key fields. In the *patient_info* table you will notice the primary key field and the foreign key field. As a matter of best practice, every table in a relational database should have a primary key. The ***primary key*** acts as the unique identifier for a record in the table. Each record's primary key must be unique, record by record, and must not be null (empty). Notice the `PatientId` field in the *patient_info* table. Since this field is used as the table's primary key, each and every record in the table must have unique data stored in this field. In other words, no two records may contain the same `PatientId` data.

Although there must be unique data in the primary key field (`PatientId` in this case), the other fields contain data that may be replicated in more than one record. For example, consider the `PrimaryCareDoctorId` field; if Dr. Waynewright, ID# 106547 (see the first row in Figure 7), treats multiple patients in the database, then his name and ID may show up in multiple records in the table.

NOTE

In a relational database, tables are often referred to as "relations," because they contain a set of records (rows) related to various fields (columns). Throughout this book, however, we will be using the term "table." Please refer to the Terminology Summary in Figure 5.

A *foreign key* field is a field within a table that is acting as a primary key in another table in the database. Let's suppose that in addition to our *patient_info* table there is another table in the database called *primary_care_doctors*, which uses the `PrimaryCareDoctorId` field as its primary key. In the *primary_care_doctors* table, Dr. Waynewright, with the ID# 106547, will appear in only one record. It is the overlap of various key fields among tables that facilitates the all-important relatability within the aptly named relational database. These relationships are commonly visualized using a database **schema**, also known as an **entity relationship diagram (ERD)**, which serves as a kind of blueprint for the database.

fig. 8

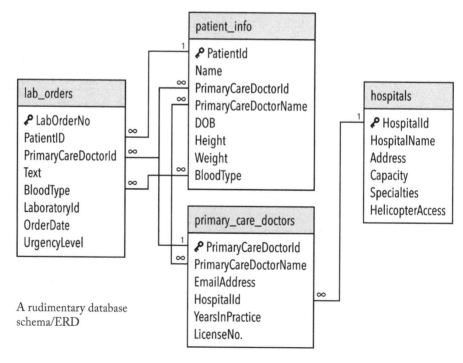

A rudimentary database
schema/ERD

For the moment, don't worry about the 1's and the ∞ symbols. We will explain them in a moment. For now, take a few minutes to study the schema and consider its relationships. There are only four tables in this schema, and the tables are connected to one another by way of one or more common fields. The `PatientId` field is the primary key for the *patient_info* table, but it is a foreign key field for the *lab_orders* table. Similarly, the `HospitalId` field is the primary key for the *hospitals* table, but it is a foreign key field for the *primary_care_doctors* table. Pretty simple, right? Let's take a look at another schema for a different kind of operation.

fig. 9

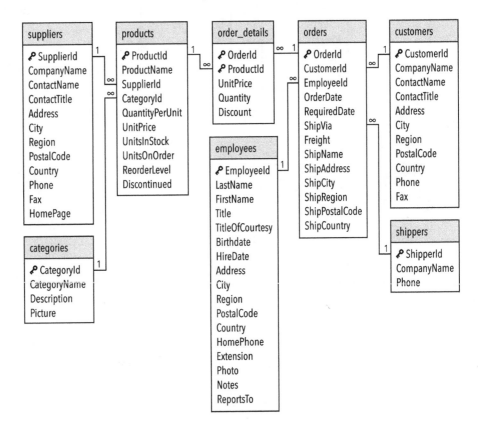

The schema in Figure 9 describes a database that handles the ordering and shipping of products to customers. Now, about those 1 and ∞ symbols found at the ends of the connecting lines in our sample schemas: these notations describe the nature of the interactivity between tables. When there is a 1 on one end of the connecting line and a ∞ symbol on the other end, it represents a "one-to-many" relationship between the tables' shared fields.

Let's take a closer look at the *products* table (Figure 10). Clearly, the data here is about various products and their attributes.

fig. 10

suppliers	products
🔑 SupplierId	🔑 ProductId
CompanyName	ProductName
ContactName	SupplierId
ContactTitle	CategoryId
Address	QuantityPerUnit
City	UnitPrice
Region	UnitsInStock
PostalCode	UnitsOnOrder
Country	ReorderLevel
Phone	Discontinued
Fax	
HomePage	

The `ProductId` field is the primary key for this table, as symbolized by the key icon. Each record in the table will contain a unique product identification number. In fact, that is the whole purpose of this table—to catalog the attributes of the database's various products.

Now, let's look at the relationship between *products* and *suppliers*.

SUPPLIERS

fig. 11

SupplierId	CompanyName	ContactName	ContactTitle	Address	City	etc.
S-101	Van Eck Industries	Bruce Davidson	Vp Operations	2158 Del Dew Drive	Temple Hills	...
S-102	Wright & Gate Co	Wilma Joy	Supply Chain Supervisor	291 Creekside Lane	Ventura	...
S-103	Olivias Supply	Brad Pence	Site Manager, Baton Rouge	4353 Locust View Drive	Baton Rouge	...
S-104	Cantor Corporation	Orville Bedford	President	2811 West Drive	Chicago	...
S-105	Bellagio Finland	Wallace Grim	Distributions Superviser	4939 Breezewood Court	Chanute	...
S-106	Decks Materials	John Tuck	VP Operations	4529 Counts Lane	Lextington	...
S-107	Lennor Co	Rachel Durst	Site Manager, Jackson	2216 Rhapsody Street	Gainesville	...

PRODUCTS

fig. 12

ProductId	ProductName	SupplierId	CategoryId	QuantityPerUnit	UnitPrice	etc.
P001	Welding goggles	S102	SA-432	1	$12.99	...
P002	Welding helmet	S102	SA-432	1	$41.49	...
P003	Stick electrodes	S104	WE-214	40	$7.00	...
P004	Magnetic clamp	S101	WE-220	1	$11.86	...
P005	Heat resistant blanket	S104	WE-212	1	$3.73	...
P006	Work table	S105	GE-100	1	$1,386.67	...
P007	Replacement plates	S105	GE-100	1	$396.00	...
P008	Welding wire	S104	WE-214	1	$112.86	...
P009	Welding coveralls	S102	SA-435	1	$60.27	...
P010	Welding nozzle	S103	WE-214	1	$141.65	...
P011	Gas regulator	S106	AU-100	1	$166.25	...
P012	Welding hoods	S102	SA-432	1	$42.37	...
P013	Spot welding electrode	S104	WE-212	1	$2.35	...
P014	Plasma cutter	S107	PL-100	1	$1,645.91	...
P015	Plasma cutter cutting tip	S107	PL-100	1	$9.27	...

There is a one-to-many relationship between *suppliers* and *products* based on the data in the `SupplierId` field. In *suppliers* each record will possess a unique identification number for each supplier, but in *products* there may be several records with the same supplier identification number.

The key icon next to the `SupplierId` field in *suppliers* alerts us to the fact that `SupplierId` is the primary key for that table. We can certainly have many different products (each with its own unique product ID number) coming from the same supplier and cataloged in the *products* table. Contrast this with *suppliers*, where we must have one and only one unique supplier ID number for each record.

GRAPHIC

fig. 13

PRODUCTS

ProductId	ProductName	SupplierId	CategoryId	QuantityPerUnit	UnitPrice	etc.
P001	Welding goggles	S102	SA-432	1	$12.99	
P002	Welding helmet	S102	SA-432	1	$41.49	
P003	Stick electrodes	S104	WE-214	40	$7.80	
P004	Magnetic clamp	S101	WE-200	1	$11.86	
P005	Heat resistant blanket	S104	WE-212	1	$3.73	
P006	Work table	S105	GE-100	1	$1,306.57	
P007	Replacement plates	S105	GE-100	1	$398.00	
P008	Welding wire	S104	WE-214	1	$117.66	
P009	Welding coveralls	S102	SA-435	1	$60.27	
P010	Welding nozzle	S103	WE-214	1	$141.65	
P011	Gas regulator	S106	AU-100	1	$166.25	
P012	Welding hoods	S102	SA-432	1	$42.37	
P013	Spot welding electrode	S104	WE-212	1	$2.35	
P014	Plasma cutter	S107	PL-100	1	$1,645.91	
P015	Plasma cutter cutting tip	S107	PL-100	1	$9.27	

SUPPLIERS

SupplierId	CompanyName	ContactName	ContactTitle	Address	City	etc.
S-101	Van Eck Industries	Bruce Davidson	Vp Operations	2158 Bell Dew Drive	Temple Hills	
S-102	Wright & Gate Co	Wilma Joy	Supply Chain Supervisor	291 Creekside Lane	Ventura	
S-103	Obrias Supply	Brad Pierce	Site Manager, Baton Rouge	4353 Locust View Drive	Baton Rouge	
S-104	Carter Corporation	Orville Beaford	President	2811 West Drive	Chicago	
S-105	Bellagre Finland	Wallace Grim	Distributions Supervisor	4939 Breezewood Court	Chanute	
S-106	Darla Materials	John Duck	VP Operations	4529 Counts Lane	Lexington	
S-107	Landud Co	Rachel Durst	Site Manager, Jackson	2216 Rhapsody Street	Gainesville	

NOTE

Identical `supplierId` data may appear in multiple records in the *products* table but not in the *suppliers* table.

Next, let's look at the relationship between the *products*, *order_details*, and *orders* tables (Figure 14).

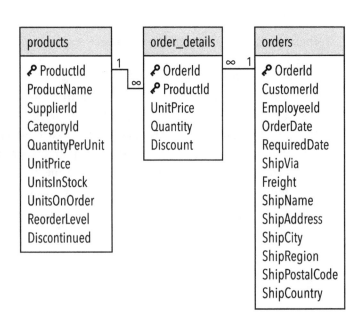

fig. 14

The *order_details* table appears to have two primary keys, as signified by the key icons. It is helpful to think of this scenario as a composite primary key, or **composite key**, whereby two or more fields are used to define the primary key. Though there are technically two keys in play, it is still best thought of as a single item—*the* primary key.

COMPOSITE KEY

fig. 15

OrderId	ProductId	UnitPrice	Quantity	Discount
101	P006	$1,386.67	1	NULL
101	P003	$7.00	3	NULL
101	P005	$3.73	1	10%
102	P011	$166.23	1	NULL
102	P013	$2.35	1	NULL
103	P014	$1,645.91	1	NULL
104	P001	$12.99	3	NULL
104	P012	$42.37	3	NULL
104	P011	$166.23	2	10%
104	P003	$7.00	5	NULL
105	P010	$141.65	1	NULL
105	P004	$11.86	3	NULL
105	P003	$7.00	2	NULL
106	P014	$1,645.91	1	NULL

The combination of data that populates the fields used to form a composite key acts as the unique identifier for any given record within the table. In other words, if the `OrderId` of a record in the *order_details* table is "101" and the `ProductId` for the same record is "P006," then we can assume that no other record in the table will have the same combination of data in those two fields. There may be one or several other records with an `OrderId` of "101," and there may one or several other records with a `ProductId` of "P006," but only one record may have both "101" as its `OrderId` *and* "P006" as its `ProductId`. This combination of data across fields acts as the composite key, which, like any primary key, provides a unique identifier for each and every record in the table.

You may have noticed that the standard primary key in any given table usually represents the "one" in a one-to-many relationship. For example, in *orders*, we can see that the primary key, the `OrderId` field, will provide a unique identifier for each record in the table. The "many" side of the relationship is found in *order_details*. Why do you think that is?

Let's think this through logically. We can infer that the purpose of *order_details* is to provide information about various products that are ordered. We can infer that any given product may be ordered multiple times by multiple customers under many different circumstances, with different prices, etc. Hence, `ProductId` cannot be used on its own as a primary key for *order_details*. We may also infer that any given order may include multiple products, and if we look at the other fields used in *order_details*—`UnitPrice`, `Quantity`, and `Discount`—then we can see clearly that these fields speak to the properties of an individual product, not an order at large. Therefore, `OrderId` cannot be used on its own as a primary key for *order_details*. The solution is to combine `ProductId` and `OrderId` into a composite key, thereby ensuring that the data contained in the `UnitPrice`, `Quantity`, and `Discount` columns corresponds to a unique and specific order *and* a unique and specific product within that order.

Types of Data

Earlier in this chapter we introduced the concept of metadata, which is data that describes limitations or formatting specifications for other data within the database. When developing a database using SQL, a specific **data type** must be designated for each and every column used. Data types will vary slightly depending on the version of SQL you are using. In general, though, you will have numeric data types, character or text-based data types, dates and times, and Boolean values. Let's talk a little bit about each of these.

Numeric Data Types

Numeric data includes integers, which are whole numbers that do not use decimals. Usually, when an integer data type is used, it comes with some form of limitation on its length. Recall that in Figure 7, the table contained data about various patients. For the Weight column we might consider assigning an integer data type with a limit of three digits. Why? Because a) we are okay rounding up or down to the nearest pound or kilogram and do not need to use decimal places, so integers will do. And b) it is inconceivable that we would need more than three digits to describe someone's weight in pounds. When integer data will not do, and we need a more precise numeric format, we can use decimal data, which will allow us to use decimals as needed to fine-tune our numeric values. Like integer data, decimal data can also be length-restricted.

NUMERIC DATA

INTEGER	DECIMAL
5	30.5
6176	14.65
47261	5.634
531	365.1
90	0.437
1	15347.45

GRAPHIC

fig. 16

NOTE

Data types that permit longer spans of digits, characters, etc., require more bytes of storage space. SQL also allows monetary numeric data types.

Character or Text-Based Data Types

Character or text-based data types may be configured to hold both a fixed-length string of characters and a variable-length string. For example, if one of your database columns included standard six-character Canadian postal codes (which include both numbers and letters), then you would use a character or text-based data type configured for a fixed-length string of six characters. If you were creating a column to hold a customer's first or last name, then you would want to configure a variable-length string using reasonable maximum and minimum length limits.

CHARACTER and TEXT-BASED DATA

fig. 17

CanadianZipCode	FirstName	LastName
L4K8R3	Ronald	Dalton
V0S0N2	Clara	Abramson
H7L9N0	Joseph	Scalia
L3M0L7	Benjamin	Dreadnaught
E6K5T8	Harold	Mercedes
E7K3C5	James	Rockefeller

The examples we have used thus far have featured relatively short text-based data, such as names and address information. Many databases contain text-based fields that permit much lengthier strings of text and characters. Some database structures can allow for the text of multipage memorandums or even books to be cataloged.

Dates and Times

Dates and times are obviously important data in many circumstances. SQL allows users to choose from a variety of different date-and-time layouts: YYYY-MM-DD, YYYY-MM-DD HH:MI:SS, YY-MM-DD. You may also format a column to hold just the year, either in a four- or two-digit format; that is, "2019" or just "19." Figure 18 exemplifies date and time data in use.

DATE and TIME DATA

DateOfBirth	CreditCardExpiration	TimeOfDelivery
01/25/1977	08/2023	2019-04-21 08:25;55
09/30/2003	05/2025	2020-12-05 13:30;15
08/15/1999	01/2023	2020-05-10 22:20;36
02/25/1962	11/2022	2019-01-17 10:20;01
09/12/1998	05/2026	2021-06-29 15:21;59
11/03/1959	03/2023	2022-09-03 16:42;26

GRAPHIC

fig. 18

NOTE

Date/time formats in SQL have built-in numeric values that allow the database to interpret requests for chronologically specific outputs. For example, if you want to know how many customers bought a certain product between the dates of October 1, 2020, and December 31, 2020, then SQL can help you generate and sort this output.

Boolean Values

A **Boolean** value is data expressed as either True or False. If you are in charge of a sensitive operation for a government or private entity, then you may use a database to help you keep track of your staff members' security clearance levels. If you need to locate a list of staff members who have security clearances A, B, and D, but not necessarily C, then using Boolean data analysis can make life easier. Figure 19 shows Boolean data in use.

NOTE

Different versions of SQL will have different lists of recognizable data types. Some versions of SQL, such as SQL Server and MySQL (discussed later in this chapter), do not provide the user with the option to label a data type as "Boolean." Instead, they provide a "Bit" data type, which can easily be appropriated into a quintessential Boolean format.

BOOLEAN DATA

fig. 19

ClearedForTakeOff	InDefault	ConvictedFelon
True	False	False
False	True	False
False	False	False
True	True	True
False	True	False

Relational Database Management Systems

SQL operates in a wide variety of software packages known as *relational database management systems (RDBMSs)*. These systems facilitate the application of SQL when one is issuing commands and posing questions to a database. Popular RDBMS software includes Oracle Database, Microsoft SQL Server, MySQL, IBM Db2, and SQLite.

fig. 20

It is not uncommon for the RDBMS software itself to be referred to as a database. This is a slight misnomer. More precisely stated, the RDBMS provides an interface (usually known as an SQL browser) for the user to interact with the data stored on the database.

Some RDBMSs are primarily graphic by design. Others are more text-based. RDBMSs also vary in their approach to SQL. We referenced one such anomaly previously in this chapter with regard to the handling of Boolean data. RDBMSs do vary in the way they present database information.

The fact that we are telling the RDBMS what information to present to us defines SQL as a "declarative" programming language. This stands in contrast to other programming languages you may be familiar with, such as C++, Java, etc. Those languages are more procedural, in that they handle creating and running a program from start to finish (allocating memory, including existing reference files, etc.). With SQL, all of the memory allocation and other procedural duties are handled by the RDBMS.

The SELECT Statement

As you know, SQL stands for structured query language, and for several decades it has set the standard for how we communicate with relational databases. The most common SQL command is SELECT, a command we will be working with quite closely in chapter 4 and throughout the rest of this book. An SQL query is usually comprised of the SELECT keyword in combination with other SQL keywords and references to the data involved in the query. As is the case in other programming languages, the correct sequence and choice of SQL keywords is vital to creating a query that can be correctly interpreted by the SQL browser. This mandated structure is also known as the *syntax* of a query.

In the following example, we can see how syntax of a query varies slightly from one RDBMS implementation to another. These are two very basic queries that essentially do the same thing (they return the first ten records from the *Products* table) but as you can see, they are phrased slightly differently.

In SQL Server we would type the following:

```
SELECT TOP 10 *
FROM
    products;
```

But in MySQL, we would type

```
SELECT *
FROM
    products
LIMIT 10;
```

If we were to structure a query in MySQL similar to the SQL Server example, the SQL browser would generate a *syntax error* which would prevent the query from running. In this case, the only difference between these two

SQL implementations is the way we tell the SQL browser to limit our results to the top ten. The rest of the query is the same. The variations between RDBMSs are generally very minor, usually less than a 10 percent change from one to another. The simple, declarative nature of SQL is fairly consistent across most RDBMSs. Therefore, if you commit yourself to learning the underlying logic of SQL within the confines of any given RDBMS, then you will find your knowledge to be quite portable; that is, you will be able to quickly tailor your knowledge of SQL fundamentals to another RDBMS.

Queries, Statements, Clauses, and Keywords

If you have had any previous experience with SQL, you may have heard these four words used interchangeably: query, statement, clause, and keyword. SELECT is a special keyword in SQL, but it is also referred to as a SELECT statement, the SELECT clause, or a SELECT query. So what is the difference? Let's start with the broadest term and finish with the most specific.

In its most basic form, a *query* is a request that returns information from the database in the form of records. A query can be composed of several SQL statements (which we will encounter in chapter 8 in the form of subqueries). An SQL *statement* is any valid piece of code that is executed by the RDBMS. The code examples we just compared are both valid SQL statements (since the RDBMS allows us to execute them) and queries (since they return a record set). A *clause* is a subsection of a query, containing at least one *keyword* and the relevant information to be used in conjunction with that keyword (in this case references to fields and tables).

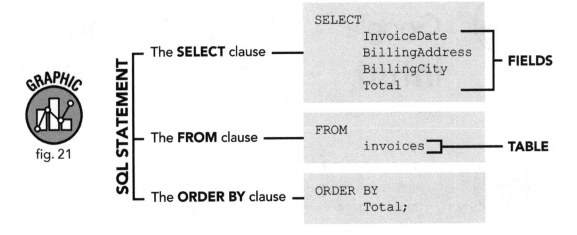

fig. 21

Words in ALL CAPS are SQL keywords.

As you can see in Figure 21, an SQL statement can be comprised of many clauses, each containing at least one keyword, as well as references to fields and tables.

As with the previous example, Figure 21 is both a complete SQL statement and a complete query. A query can contain multiple clauses, each starting with a keyword.

Introducing SQLite

Now that we have a basic grasp of database architecture and how we interact with it, let's switch gears a bit and move toward a more hands-on learning approach using real-world problem-solving scenarios. As we mentioned, there are several different RDBMSs to choose from. It would be ineffective in this context to try to go function by function, documenting the nuances of each individual RDBMS. Instead, we have selected SQLite as the official RDBMS of this book. SQLite is a very accessible and practical choice for new learners. It is an open-source software product and thus free to use for any purpose. About 99 percent of what you learn using SQLite is applicable to most other RDBMSs. SQLite is also one of the most widely used RDBMS systems in the world—used in computers, mobile devices, even automobiles.[9] More information and some additional documentation can be found at https://www.sqlite.org/index.html.

fig. 22

Some of the well-known companies that use SQLite.

The "Lite" in SQLite does not refer to the capabilities of this software, but rather to the fact that it is *lightweight* when it comes to setup complexity, administrative overhead, and resource usage.

Chapter Recap

» A table is a two-dimensional grid of rows and columns that contains data.

» Data can exist as a variety of different data types, such as strings of text, numbers, or special characters.

» Metadata describes the nature and format of the data, including any minimum/maximum character length or required numbers, letters, or special characters.

» Relational databases can contain many tables. Each table in a relational database should have a primary key that serves as a unique identifier for that table.

» A foreign key is any column in a table that exists as primary key in another table.

» The relationship between tables and their primary and foreign keys is called the database schema and can be shown visually by an entity relationship diagram (ERD), which functions as a blueprint for the database.

» There are a variety of different relational database management systems (RDBMSs) such as Oracle Database, Microsoft SQL Server, MvSQL, IBM Db2, and SQLite. Though they differ in many ways, all share the structured query language as a backbone.

» The SELECT keyword is the most common SQL command used in SQL queries.

» SQL statements can contain multiple clauses using different SQL keywords.

» This text will use SQLite, but the skills you learn here can easily translate to other RDBMS platforms.

| 2 |
SQL Tools and Strategies

Chapter Overview
- » Setting up our SQL environment
- » The sTunes database
- » DB Browser for SQLite
- » Self-assessments
- » SQL learning strategies

So far, we have talked a bit about what a relational database is, how data is structured inside of a database, and how we can use a relational database management system (RDBMS) to ask questions of the database (by writing queries) and obtain meaningful results. Now that we have gone over the fundamental concepts and terminology, we need to set up a working SQL environment so that we can start practicing queries. This chapter will familiarize you with the resources intended to be used in conjunction with this book, as well as the many exercises and self-assessment questions that will help you test your SQL knowledge.

Introducing the sTunes Database

Imagine you were just hired as an SQL data analyst by an online retail music company, to perform analysis on their music sales data. You are given access to the company database and told it contains product information (in this case, songs and albums), personal customer information, employee records, and sales data. Management wants to know if the data in the sTunes database contains any useful information about sales, customer demographics, and any ways the company can improve or expand their services. You are given the task of analyzing their database and presenting to management any insights you discover about the data. You perform all your analysis with SQL. To begin this task, you will need to download a copy of this database onto your computer.

Introducing DB Browser for SQLite

As we mentioned at the end of chapter 1, we will be working with an RDBMS called SQLite, pronounced "SQL Lite." Although SQLite is the particular implementation or protocol for our sample database, we still need to download an actual application (also known as an SQL browser) that we can use to "browse" our database just like a web browser is used to interpret pages on the web. SQLite comes with *DB Browser*, which is a high-quality, visual, open-source tool used to create, design, and edit database files compatible with SQLite. It is for users and developers wanting to create databases, search, and edit data.

Installing DB Browser for SQLite

To install DB Browser, follow the download link included in the digital assets located at www.clydebankmedia.com/sql-assets. Once there, you will find a variety of download links for different operating systems. Be sure to choose the operating system that is relevant to you (32- or 64-bit Windows, Mac OS, Linux, etc.). After downloading the correct file, navigate to where you downloaded it and install the software.

How to Test Your SQL Knowledge

As with any technical skill, practice is the key to mastery. Besides providing examples from a sample database, this book features two types of exercises in the following chapters to assess your newly acquired knowledge of SQL. Exercises labeled "ON YOUR OWN" allow you to quickly practice your skills immediately after a new concept is introduced. As the name implies, these questions do not have written solutions but are not intended to be overly difficult. Another form of self-assessment are the "Data Analysis Checkpoints." These exercises are more challenging and may require knowledge of concepts explained in previous chapters. You can find detailed solutions to every Data Analysis Checkpoint in Appendix I.

Strategies for Success

Before we launch our software and open up the sTunes Database, I'd like to offer a few words of advice, to beginner and expert alike. These words come from my experience as a teacher, and following this advice will greatly improve your chances of success:

Type Out Every Code Example by Hand

If you have access to a digital version of this text, do not just copy and paste coding examples into the SQL browser! This advice applies especially to the beginning student who has not experienced SQL before. I am very against the idea that you can learn a programming language by merely copying existing code examples or exercises into the RDBMS environment and observing what they do. Copying and pasting bypasses the syntax, spelling, and muscle memory you activate by rewriting the query yourself. Pasting code from other sources can introduce formatting errors in your code that are difficult to diagnose. For example, pasting code that includes word-processor-formatted quotation marks will often cause a syntax error because DB Browser does not interpret these symbols as single quotation marks. The mistakes we make are just as important as the successes. If the SQL statement you are trying to execute results in a bizarre syntax error, sometimes the best thing to do is delete everything and write the query again from scratch.

Convert SQL Queries to Natural Language Questions

When answering a question or writing a query, try to think of the result as an answer to a real-world question. Instead of thinking "How many entries are in the customers table?" think "How many customers do we have?" This book is intended to help start or enhance your career using SQL as a tool in your ever-expanding toolbox. The questions you will get from your managers and coworkers will be real-world questions, so it's important to learn the technique of turning a real-world question into an SQL statement and then back into a real-world answer.

Treat This Book Like a Reference Guide

We realize that some of our readers will already have some familiarity with SQL and may want to jump ahead to a particular section. We have designed this book to include the SQL keywords (discussed in each chapter) within the chapter headings so that our readers can easily navigate through the text or quickly go back to review a concept they have already learned. In addition to quick navigation aids, we have included a second appendix with a list of SQL keywords by chapter and some stand-alone examples to get you writing queries as soon as possible. We hope you will keep this book by your desk and refer to it as often as you need to.

Although topic jumping is encouraged, we recommend reading the next chapter (3) first, as it will introduce the software needed to run all of the example queries in the remainder of the book.

Chapter Recap

» This book is designed to introduce the minimum required background information and then jump right in to writing SQL queries.

» To achieve this goal, and to get the most out of this book, it must be used concurrently with database software up and running as well as a sample database.

» As a data analyst, you will often be given an existing database to analyze. The sTunes database file provided here serves as a good example of what an existing database will look like when you first open it.

» DB Browser for SQLite is a free-to-use, public domain database software program that is lightweight and is a good starting point for learning how to examine database files. This program can be run in a Windows or macOS environment.

» Two types of self-assessments are provided in this text to help test your knowledge. The answers to the Data Analysis Checkpoints can be found in Appendix I.

» To make the most of your learning experience, type out the SQL queries in this book by hand (instead of copying them) and consider any SQL question in terms of its real-world meaning.

| 3 |
Exploring a Database in SQLite

Chapter Overview

- » Launching the SQL software
- » Opening a database file
- » The Database Structure tab
- » The Browse Data tab
- » The Execute SQL tab
- » Viewing query results
- » Data Analysis Checkpoint

In this chapter, we will familiarize ourselves with the interface of our chosen SQL browser for SQLite: DB Browser.

Environment Orientation

We have a bit more preparation to do and then we are ready to start analyzing the sTunes database. Now that we have installed DB Browser for SQLite software and downloaded the sTunes sample database, it is time to fire it up and get going!

1. Start the DB Browser for SQLite application.
   a. **Mac users**: Go to Finder and double-click DB Browser for SQLite in your Applications folder.
   b. **Windows users**: Go to your Start Menu and click on the DB Browser for SQLite application from your list of installed programs.

2. You will see the following default screen (Figure 23):

fig. 23

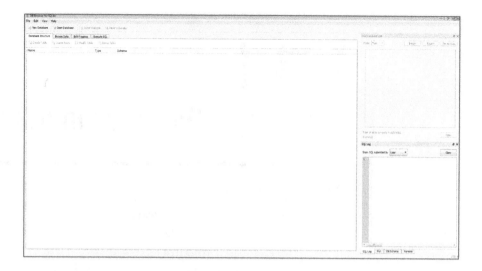

Opening the sTunes Database

3. With DB Browser open, click on "Open Database."

fig. 24

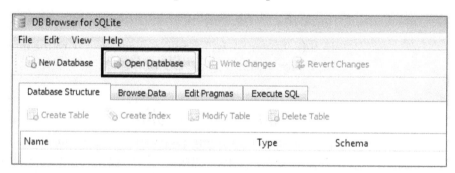

4. This opens the "Choose a Database File" dialog box. Navigate to the folder where you downloaded the sTunes sample database file and click on "Open."

fig. 25

Investigating the Structure of the Database

When the file is opened, the Database Structure tab shows the tables contained in the sample database.

fig. 26

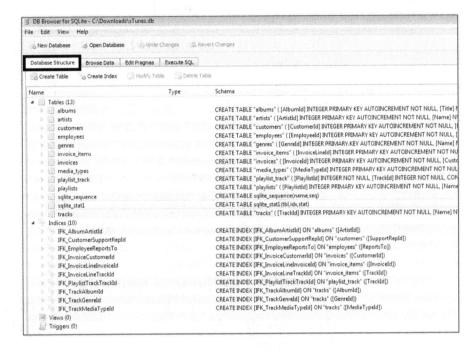

Now that we can investigate the database structure, we can learn a lot more about our fictitious company, sTunes. Once the IT department gives us the proper permissions, our company will most likely give us some time to familiarize ourselves with the database we were tasked to analyze. Before we start writing any SQL statements, it's a good idea to see what type of data we have available to us.

First, we can see that there are thirteen tables in the sTunes database. By expanding the arrow to the left of the table name, we are shown the fields contained in each table. In the *albums* table, as can be seen in Figure 27, the fields are `AlbumId`, `Title`, and `ArtistId`.

fig. 27

At the beginning of chapter 1, we talked about the fundamental terminology of this book. The fields we are seeing are the columns in each table. The data stretched across the rows of the table (not pictured here) are the records.

The `AlbumId` field is an *integer* data type, which means it holds numeric data (numbers).

The `Title` field is a character data type (known as `NVARCHAR`), which means it holds characters or non-numeric data.

The `ArtistId` field is also an integer data type.

We spoke about metadata and different data types in chapter 1, where we went over database structure. The `Type` field in our database browser panel (see Figure 27) is a good example of metadata. The data type for each field is chosen based on the most logical type for its function.

Viewing the Individual Records

The Browse Data tab can be used to see the records contained in each table. Use the drop-down to switch between tables and browse the data contained in each one.

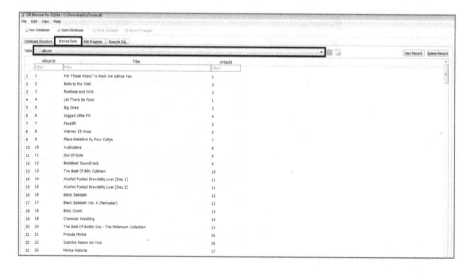

fig. 28

In Figure 28, the Browse Data tab displays the data stored in the *albums* table. It shows the columns we observed in the Database Structure tab. It also shows the actual data contained in these columns.

In row 1, the following data is contained in each column of the *albums* table:

```
AlbumId = 1
Title = "For Those About to Rock We Salute You"
ArtistId = 1
```

As per our chapter 1 terminology discussion, the columns you are seeing are referred to as fields. Every row represents an individual record.

By examining this table, we can also learn a bit about the other tables in this database. In chapter 1, we introduced the concept of a foreign key field. In this table we can see that the primary key is `AlbumId` (there is a unique number for each record). We also have an `ArtistId` which accepts an integer instead of an actual artist name. This gives us a hint that there is probably another table that holds the actual artist name as a character data type and that `ArtistId` is most likely a foreign key field.

A foreign key is a field that exists as a primary key in another table. If we look at the *artists* table, we can confirm that `ArtistId` is the primary key in that table, so it exists as a foreign key in this one.

The Execute SQL Tab

The Execute SQL tab is where you write your SQL statements. There are three main component window panes in the execute SQL tab: the **Query Pane**, the **Results Pane**, and the **Messages Pane**. Let's explore these three panes by writing the following SQL code into the Query Pane, as seen in Figure 29:

```
SELECT
    *
FROM
    albums;
```

This SQL statement selects all fields (the * symbol designates "all fields") from the *albums* table and, once you press the play button above the Query Pane, displays the fields, and data in those fields, in the Results Pane below.

As seen in Figure 29, the Play button to the left executes all SQL statements written in the window. The Play button to the right executes only the SQL statement that your cursor is on (it executes only one statement at a time).

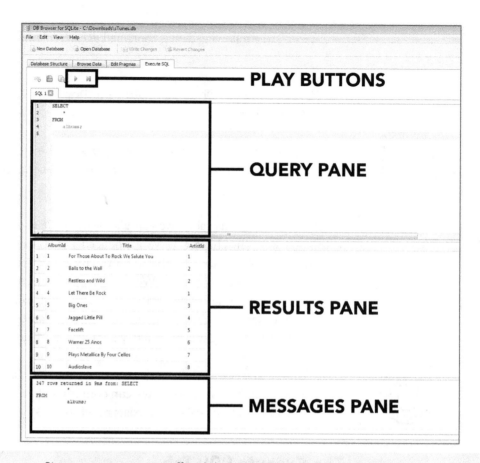

PLAY BUTTONS

QUERY PANE

RESULTS PANE

MESSAGES PANE

fig. 29

Since we are starting off with basic queries, we are only going to be running one SQL statement at a time. More advanced queries can use multiple statements executed at the same time. The ability to execute statements individually is valuable in multi-statement queries. If you have only one complete SQL statement in the Execute Pane, then these Play buttons essentially do the same thing.

The Results Pane lists the output generated by our query. If we have more results than can be viewed on the screen at one time (Figure 30), the browser provides us with a scroll bar to navigate down through all the results.

There is another way to determine if what we see on the screen (in this case only five results), represents the entire query or if there is more data available. Under the Results Pane is the Messages Pane, which displays informative messages about our query.

> » The number of rows returned from our SQL statement
> » How much time our query or SQL statement took to run
> » Error messages, if our SQL statement contained errors

	AlbumId	Title	ArtistId	
1	1	For Those About To Rock We Salute You	1	
2	2	Balls to the Wall	2	
3	3	Restless and Wild	2	
4	4	Let There Be Rock	1	
5	5	Big Ones	3	

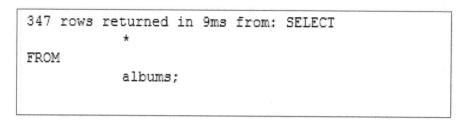

```
347 rows returned in 9ms from: SELECT
                 *
FROM
           albums;
```

The first thing we see is that our query returned 347 rows of data. If we did not notice the scroll bar, then this message would serve as our notification to scroll down. The second thing we observe is that our query was returned in 9 milliseconds (abbreviated as 9ms). You may wonder why it is valuable to see how much time it takes to process a query. In this case, it doesn't really tell us anything. However, in larger databases with more advanced queries, it can take much longer to return data. The length of time it takes also depends on how a database is optimized and structured. We will talk more about database structure in chapter 6 when working with multiple tables.

The Messages Pane is also the location where any error messages will be displayed. If your query does not execute correctly, check the Messages Pane.

Data Analysis Checkpoint

You have reached the first Data Analysis Checkpoint in this book! These checkpoints will be at the end of every remaining chapter. This is a good time to practice what you have learned so far.

Using the Database Structure tab and the Browse Data tab, try to answer the following questions:

1. How many tables are in our database?

2. How many fields does the table named *tracks* have?

   9

3. What are some of the data types in this table?

   INTERGER / NVARCHAR

4. What does the actual data look like in the table?

   NUMBERS + LETTERS

REMEMBER

The answers to these Data Analysis Checkpoints are at the end of the book in Appendix I.

Chapter Recap

» DB Browser for SQLite, the chosen software for this text, opens like any other computer software program.

» Selecting the Open Database button will allow you to select a database file from your computer to open.

» Investigate the structure of the database file with the Database Structure tab.

» Use the Browse Data tab to view individual records in the table you select with the provided drop-down menu.

» Use the Execute SQL tab to write and then execute your first SQL statement.

» The Results Pane contains the data returned by your query.

» The Messages Pane contains information about your query including how many rows were returned, how long the query took to run, and any applicable error messages.

PART II

WRITING SQL STATEMENTS

| 4 |
Getting Started with Queries

SQL is a powerful and robust language that offers the user a wide variety of commands. Although there are more commands than we could ever show in this book, there are a few simple and easy-to-use commands that we can start experimenting with immediately. This chapter will cover the basics of writing a good query and formatting the results. By the end of this chapter you will be able to select individual fields from a specific database and display those fields in alphabetical order. Let's get started!

Adding Comments to Queries

Before we begin composing our first SQL query, we will take a look at creating comments. Comments are plain English sentences used to help add insight and authoring information about SQL statements that you create. It is considered an industry best practice to use comments in your SQL queries; they help both the SQL author and those that come after the author to quickly gain understanding and context regarding the intention and function of the given SQL statement.

There are two ways to create a comment. Preceding anything written in the Query Pane with two hyphens (--) creates a comment on that line. Our example shows a comment created on line 1 (Figure 32).

A comment block is a multi-line comment. It is created using the front slash and star symbols to open the block /*, followed by a star and a front slash */, which closes the block. Anything that falls between the opening and closing symbols becomes part of the comment (Figure 33).

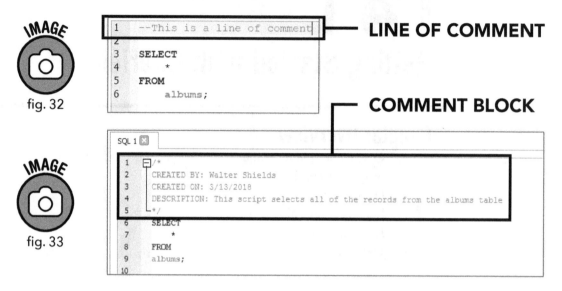

fig. 32

LINE OF COMMENT

COMMENT BLOCK

fig. 33

Our example shows some standard information that is very useful to include in a comment block. The author, date, and description provide significant value to anyone who encounters the SQL query or script.

MY TAKE

Comments are often overlooked completely in SQL texts. We omit comments in future chapters for the sake of brevity only. When working with real-world databases, preexisting comments have saved me a lot of time that I would have otherwise spent writing additional queries to figure out how the database functioned. Comments become especially important when your queries will be read or used by others.

The Structure of a Basic Query

Writing a query is like asking a question in any natural language. The phrasing matters, the details matter, and the order of the words matters. The more detailed our question is, the more precise our answer will be.

In the creation of an SQL query, we need to consider the following five questions:

1. What database are we speaking to?
2. What table within that database are we requesting data from?
3. What fields within that table are we interested in?

4. Do we want to exclude any data, filter or omit any range or time period?
5. In one concise sentence, what does our query do?

The purpose of the foregoing questions is to help us build a bridge between the natural language we use every day and the language of SQL. If you are employed as a data analyst, you will be asked normal questions from your boss or coworkers about the business. You will have to convert these plain-language questions into SQL statements in order to answer them. After you have received the results of your query, you will then have to convert those results back into natural language that is accessible to all. Such is the nature of the job.

If you are having trouble with a query, refer to the five questions above. Contemplating these questions will help you write your query.

Start Writing Your Query

To begin writing your first query, you can use the existing Execute SQL tab labeled "SQL 1" or start a new Query Pane tab, in the same way that you would open a new web browser tab. Click on the "Open Tab" icon.

fig. 34

With our new Query Pane opened, the first thing we will write is a comment block:

```
/*
CREATED BY: <your name>
CREATED ON: <date>
DESCRIPTION: <A concise description of your query,
i.e., question #5>
*/
```

After finishing our comment block, we can begin to write our first SQL statement. But to do that, we need a good question to answer. In chapter 2, we introduced the concept of an operational scenario for this book: imagining yourself as a data analyst for the fictional company sTunes. As you have seen from exploring the sTunes database in chapter 3, sTunes sells online music and has a digital library of artists, tracks, and albums and a list of customers who have purchased these songs. Let's say sTunes customer service wants to send a new promotional advertisement to all existing customers. Customer service wants to know if their customer contact list is up to date, so they ask us if we can get a complete list of first names, last names, and customer email addresses (if available) from the database. How would we go about answering this question? Let's start by answering the questions listed earlier in the chapter.

1. **What database are we speaking to?**

In this case, we are dealing with only one database. The sTunes database should already be opened in DB Browser. If you have closed the browser since working through chapter 3, you may need to open it and the sTunes database file again.

2. **What table within that database are we requesting data FROM?**

We are looking for customer information. Browsing our Database Structure tab, we can see that we have a table named customers. That table looks promising.

3. **What fields within that table are we SELECTing to display?**

This question can be answered by our Browse Data tab. If we click on that tab and select the customers table in our drop-down menu, we see that it has fields for first name, last name, and email.

4. **Do we want to exclude any data, filter or omit any range or time period?**

In this case, sTunes customer service wants a list of all customers, so we'd better not omit anything.

5. **In one concise sentence, what does our query do?**

This query selects the first name, last name, and email address from the customers table.

After adding your comment block, start by typing FROM customers. This tells your query what table to look in for its data. Then type the keyword

SELECT above the FROM clause, followed by the names of the fields within the *customers* table that you wish to view. Each field name is separated by a comma. The comma tells SQL to expect another field. The resulting code should look like this:

```
/*
CREATED BY: Walter Shields
CREATED ON: 3/13/2018
DESCRIPTION: This query selects the first name,
last name, and email from the customers table.
*/

SELECT
    FirstName,
    LastName,
    Email
FROM
    customers;
```

After composing this SQL query, run the statement by clicking on the Execute SQL play button in the menu bar. The results of the query are displayed in the Results Pane below (Figure 35). The Messages Pane also shows that the query returned 59 rows (aka records) in 3 milliseconds.

fig. 35

ON YOUR OWN:

» Add another field from the *customers* table to this query. Try adding the Company or Phone field to our sTunes mailing list. Don't forget to add an extra comma!

Coding Syntax Versus Coding Convention

As we mentioned in chapter 1, all queries must conform to a certain syntax in order to be understood by the SQL browser. When writing queries, there is much more to take into consideration than just making sure the SQL browser can understand you. It is also important that other database users can understand and follow your queries. The practice of writing queries in a standardized, readable, and consistent way is known as *coding convention*. Coding conventions vary in different database environments. This section will explain the coding conventions used in this book.

In earlier examples of queries, we used a * symbol after our SELECT keyword (in lieu of specifying individual fields). This special symbol tells the SQL browser to retrieve and display all fields in a table. Although this symbol is useful in some circumstances, in most cases it is a best practice to determine which fields you specifically want to select and call out those fields by name.

The semicolon at the end of the statement is optional in this case, since we are only writing one single SQL statement. The semicolon denotes the end of an SQL statement. Since most of the SQL queries we will be writing in this book are single statements, we will be omitting the semicolon from this point forward.

In the SELECT clause, we have chosen three fields to display. We must separate every field with a comma (except for after the last field). Omitting a comma between fields or adding a comma after the last field are both common syntax mistakes that will result in a syntax error appearing in your query Results Pane.

Notice that the code is broken up on multiple lines. We could write the entire query all on one line and the SQL browser would still recognize the code and return results. But it is a best practice to separate queries into clauses with the content of each clause indented on a new line. Later in this text, our queries will become much longer and will contain many more clauses. Organizing our queries with indents and spacing increases readability and helps others to follow along.

A clause is a subsection of an SQL statement that starts with a special SQL keyword (SELECT, FROM, etc.) and may include additional parameters and operators.

Adding an Alias to Your Columns

Often the technical language of the database will differ from the common language of a business. Sometimes you will be working with old databases or those that have not had their field names updated in a while. If you apply an **alias** to a field name (in order to describe the data in a way your coworkers are more likely to understand), any report you deliver will make much more sense to both you and anyone else reading along. Using aliases is also helpful if you want to clean up the column names and make your query output more readable or aesthetically pleasing.

In the following example, we will demonstrate several different ways to create an alias for selected field names from our *customers* table. An alias is always listed directly after the name of a field from our database. Aliases are commonly associated with the AS keyword, however, the use of the AS keyword between the field name and the alias name is optional in most RDBMS implementations.

```
/*
CREATED BY: Walter Shields
CREATED ON: 3/13/2018
DESCRIPTION: This query selects the first name,
last name, email, and phone number fields from the
customers table and demonstrates four different
ways to create an alias.
*/

SELECT
    FirstName AS 'First Name',
    LastName AS [Last Name],
    Email AS EMAIL
    Phone CELL
FROM
    customers
```

As seen in the preceding query, we used the AS keyword for the first three fields, then omitted this keyword for the Phone field, which we renamed to CELL. If the alias you create contains multiple words (such as First Name and Last Name), it needs to be surrounded with some sort of demarcation, in this case either single quotes '' or square brackets [] as shown. Since the aliases EMAIL and CELL are single words, they don't need any quotations or brackets.

SQL allows a great deal of variation in alias syntax. Other RDBMSs may not recognize every aliasing method listed here. If you get a syntax error when running your query, check to see how you designated your alias.

WITHOUT ALIASES

	FirstName	LastName	Email	Phone
1	Luís	Gonçalves	luisg@embraer.com.br	+55 (12) 3923-5555
2	Leonie	Köhler	leonekohler@surfeu.de	+49 0711 2842222
3	François	Tremblay	ftremblay@gmail.com	+1 (514) 721-4711
4	Bjørn	Hansen	bjorn.hansen@yahoo.no	+47 22 44 22 22
5	František	Wichterlová	frantisekw@jetbrains.com	+420 2 4172 5555
6	Helena	Holý	hholy@gmail.com	+420 2 4177 0449
7	Astrid	Gruber	astrid.gruber@apple.at	+43 01 5134505
8	Daan	Peeters	daan_peeters@apple.be	+32 02 219 03 03
9	Kara	Nielsen	kara.nielsen@jubii.dk	+453 3331 9991
10	Eduardo	Martins	eduardo@woodstock.com.br	+55 (11) 3033-5446

WITH ALIASES

	First Name	Last Name	EMAIL	CELL
1	Luís	Gonçalves	luisg@embraer.com.br	+55 (12) 3923-5555
2	Leonie	Köhler	leonekohler@surfeu.de	+49 0711 2842222
3	François	Tremblay	ftremblay@gmail.com	+1 (514) 721-4711
4	Bjørn	Hansen	bjorn.hansen@yahoo.no	+47 22 44 22 22
5	František	Wichterlová	frantisekw@jetbrains.com	+420 2 4172 5555
6	Helena	Holý	hholy@gmail.com	+420 2 4177 0449
7	Astrid	Gruber	astrid.gruber@apple.at	+43 01 5134505
8	Daan	Peeters	daan_peeters@apple.be	+32 02 219 03 03
9	Kara	Nielsen	kara.nielsen@jubii.dk	+453 3331 9991
10	Eduardo	Martins	eduardo@woodstock.com.br	+55 (11) 3033-5446

IMAGE

fig. 36

As you can see in Figure 36, the output on the left leaves the field names unchanged. The output on the right shows how our aliases modified the column names. Adding an alias will not change the data in the database. Aliases only alter how fields are displayed in the Results Pane.

ON YOUR OWN:
- » Add another field to this query and give it an alias.
- » Practice changing the alias syntax and omitting the AS keyword entirely. Does this have any effect on your output?

Avoid using any existing SQL keywords as your alias names. Using existing keywords could cause confusion, generate syntax errors, or cause the RDBMS to interpret your alias as a command instead.

Using the ORDER BY Clause

In our fictional scenario, we are providing a list of customers to sTunes customer service. It might be useful to order our results by the last name of our customers. To sort our results by customer last name, we need to use a new clause after our FROM clause. The ORDER BY clause allows us to sort our query results by any field(s) we choose. The default sort order is ascending, A to Z. The special keyword ASC, which specifies ascending order, is optional. To sort in descending order (Z to A), we would add the keyword DESC after the field being sorted. ORDER BY LastName DESC would sort the aliased column FirstName in descending order.

```
/*
CREATED BY: Walter Shields
CREATED ON: 3/13/2018
DESCRIPTION: This query selects the first name,
last name, and email from the customers table,
ordered by Last Name.
*/

SELECT
    FirstName AS [First Name],
    LastName AS [Last Name],
    Email AS [EMAIL]
FROM
    customers
ORDER BY
    LastName ASC
```

IMAGE

fig. 37

NOTE

Without ORDER BY, every query will return data in the order that it was initially saved in the table.

We can use the ORDER BY clause to sort by multiple columns as well. In this example, we will sort by first name (ascending), and then by last name (descending). This will require us to list two fields in our ORDER BY clause. Just like with the SELECT clause, when listing multiple fields, we must separate them by commas.

```
/*
CREATED BY: Walter Shields
CREATED ON: 3/13/2018
DESCRIPTION: This query selects the first name,
last name, and email from the customers table,
ordered by first name (ascending), then last name
(descending).
*/

SELECT
    FirstName AS [First Name],
    LastName AS [Last Name],
    Email AS [EMAIL]
FROM
    customers
ORDER BY
    FirstName ASC,
    LastName DESC
```

fig. 38

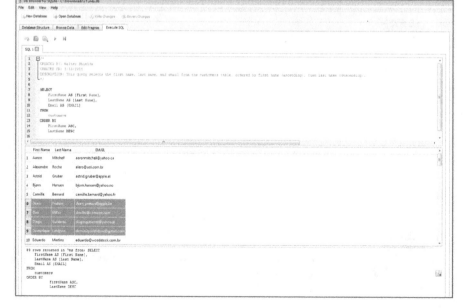

When we run this query and look at the customer first names starting with *D*, we can see that first names are in ascending order and last names are in descending order.

> If you use the ORDER BY statement on a column where some of the corresponding rows have empty values, you will see those values show up as NULL at the very top if you are using ascending order.

ON YOUR OWN:
» Rearrange the fields in the SELECT clause so that LastName is the first column instead of the second. Order the output by LastName. Does this make the list more readable?

Selecting the Top Ten Records Using **LIMIT**

In our queries so far, we have returned every record available from the *customers* table. Although we have limited our records to three fields, and sorted those fields, we can see in our Messages Pane that we are returning 59 rows every time. If we are not interested in seeing all 59 records, we can limit our results to a specified number of rows. This is often helpful when sorting queries by a number (which we will demonstrate later), like highest price or largest sale. Adding the keywords LIMIT 10 after the ORDER BY clause returns only the first ten records from the query in the sort order you specify. This number can be changed to any number you wish to limit your results by (provided there are at least that many records in the table).

```
/*
CREATED BY: Walter Shields
CREATED ON: 3/13/2018
DESCRIPTION: This query selects the first 10 records
from the customers table, ordered by first name
(ascending), then last name (descending).
*/

SELECT
    FirstName AS [First Name],
    LastName AS [Last Name],
    Email AS [EMAIL]
FROM
    customers
```

```
ORDER BY
    FirstName ASC,
    LastName DESC
LIMIT 10
```

fig. 39

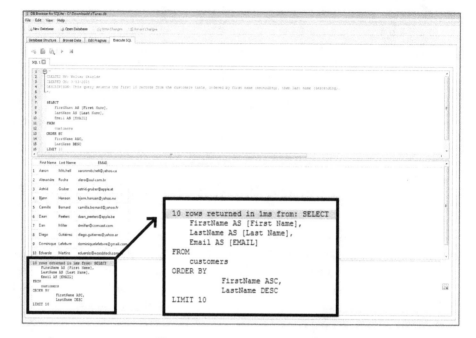

As we can see in Figure 39, our Messages Pane now says "10 rows returned in 1ms." The query performs the ORDER BY operation first and then applies the limit.

There is no requirement to use LIMIT with ORDER BY. In many cases, it makes sense to order your results by certain criteria before you limit them. If you do not use the ORDER BY clause, the results of the LIMIT statement will be returned to you in the order they were originally added to the table.

Data Analysis Checkpoint

1. How many customers' last names begin with *B*?

    4

2. When sorted in descending order, which company appears at the top in the *customers* table? WOODSTOCK DISCO$

3. How many customers do not have a postal code listed?

    4

Chapter Recap

» Adding comments to queries is considered a best practice. A basic comment block can include your name, the date the query was created, and a brief description of what the query does.

» When composing a query, it is helpful to phrase what you want in a natural language first, then decide what keywords and clauses you need.

» A basic query usually begins with a SELECT clause that specifies what fields to display from the table specified in the FROM clause.

» An alias used after the AS keyword can rename or reformat the field names in your query results. This change is only cosmetic and does not affect the data in the database.

» Using ORDER BY allows you to sort alphabetically by field(s), either in ascending (ASC) or descending (DESC) order.

» You can limit the number of results returned by using LIMIT after your ORDER BY clause. You must include the number of results you wish to show.

| 5 |
Turning Data into Information

Chapter Overview
» Operators in SQL
» The WHERE clause
» Searching for text using wildcard values
» The DATE() function
» Using OR and AND together
» The CASE statement
» Data Analysis Checkpoint

At this point in our study, using a basic SELECT statement query, we can return any set of fields from a database table and see that data ordered by the field of our choice. Displaying and ordering fields is a valuable first step in our learning journey, but we need more precise tools so that we can ask more specific questions. In the previous chapter's Data Analysis Checkpoint, we asked you how many customers' last names began with B. If you did the exercise, you noticed that the query didn't return very many names. It was easy, in this case, to sort the data alphabetically by last name and then just manually count the names ending in B. But what if our database was much larger and contained a million customers? Would you really want to manually count all the B names? Fortunately, SQL provides some tools that not only allow us to narrow down our *result set* (that is, the results of our query) to very specific data, but also to order and filter our data by user-specified conditions. Let's see what these new statements can do!

From this point on in the text, we will not be showing screen captures of the DB Browser output (unless we are specifically referring to a feature of the browser). Instead, we will be showing the output of our queries in tabular form (Figure 40).

fig. 40

Result set containing only three rows

	InvoiceDate	BillingAddress
1	1/1/2009 0:00	Theodor-Heuss-Straße 34
2	2/1/2009 0:00	Barbarossastraße 19
3	2/1/2009 0:00	8, Rue Hanovre
	3 rows returned in 3ms	

Result set containing more than three rows, but only displaying the first three

	InvoiceDate	BillingAddress
1	1/1/2009 0:00	Theodor-Heuss-Straße 34
2	2/1/2009 0:00	Barbarossastraße 19
3	2/1/2009 0:00	8, Rue Hanovre
...	150 rows returned in 3ms	

Comparison, Logical, and Arithmetic Operators

Operators are special keywords in SQL that we use in conjunction with SQL clauses to compare the values of fields, select subsets of fields, or perform arithmetic operations. Unlike the keywords we have explored already, such as SELECT, operators cannot exist as their own SQL clause but must be used with other clauses such as the SELECT clause and the WHERE clause (which we will explore in this chapter). Figure 41 shows the three types of operators we will use in this chapter.

TYPES OF OPERATORS

fig. 41

COMPARISON	LOGICAL	ARITHMETIC
= Equal To	BETWEEN	+ Add
> Greater Than	IN	- Subtract
< Less Than	LIKE	/ Divide
>= Greater Than or Equal To	AND	* Multiply
<= Less Than or Equal To	OR	% Modulo
<> Not Equal To		

These different types of operators can be combined to make more complex queries. Combining different types of operators allows us to search for ranges of data or create unique conditions. There are many more options than we can list in this chapter, but we will go over some of the more common ones.

In the following example, we can see arithmetic operators being used in conjunction with the SELECT clause to augment the value of a field called Total from the sTunes *invoices* table. Arithmetic operations are useful when we need to add taxes, surcharges, or other modifications to numeric data.

```
SELECT
    Total AS [Original Amount],
    Total + 10 AS [Addition Operator],
    Total - 10 AS [Subtraction Operator],
    Total / 10 AS [Division Operator],
    Total * 10 AS [Multiplication Operator],
    Total % 10 AS [Modulo Operator]
FROM
    invoices
ORDER BY
    Total DESC
```

GRAPHIC

fig. 42

	Original Amount	Addition Operator	Subtraction Operator	Division Operator	Multiplication Operator	Modulo Operator
1	25.86	35.86	15.86	2.586	258.6	5
2	23.86	33.86	13.86	2.386	238.6	3
3	21.86	31.86	11.86	2.186	218.6	1
4	21.86	31.86	11.86	2.186	218.6	1
5	18.86	28.86	8.86	1.886	188.6	8
...	412 results in 42ms					

ON YOUR OWN:

» Using the example query above, show the Total field from *invoices* with a 15 percent tax added.

Filtering Records by Numbers with the WHERE Clause

Other than SELECT, the most common place we will encounter operators is in the WHERE clause. The WHERE clause allows us to add specific conditions to our queries. Using WHERE, we can limit the results of our queries so that only data that satisfies our conditions appears in our result set. Some common types of data we can filter for include numbers, text, and dates. In order to filter records to return specific data, we use the WHERE clause in conjunction with operators.

In the following example, let's imagine the sales department from our fictional sTunes company asked us a question like "How many customers purchased two songs at $0.99 each?" How would we go about answering that question? In the chapter 3 Data Analysis Checkpoint, we looked at the *tracks* table. We observed that our company sells individual songs for both $0.99 and $1.99, as we can see in Figure 43.

fig. 43

If we look in the *invoices* table, as shown in Figure 44, we can see the total price of customer orders in the Total field.

fig. 44

If we wanted to see how many customers purchased just two $0.99 songs, we would look in the *invoices* table for total amounts of $1.98, which would represent two songs.

Using the tools we learned in the last chapter, we could write a query that selects all invoices and then orders them by total, but that would require us to manually count. Instead, we can insert a WHERE clause between the FROM and ORDER BY clauses to search for only those totals that equal $1.98. In conjunction with the total, adding a few other fields, such as invoice date and address, will help identify each invoice. Adding in all these clauses yields the following:

```
SELECT
    InvoiceDate,
    BillingAddress,
    BillingCity,
    Total
FROM
    invoices
WHERE
    Total = 1.98
ORDER BY
    InvoiceDate
```

fig. 45

	InvoiceDate	BillingAddress	BillingCity	Total
1	2009-01-01 00:00:00	Theodor-Heuss-Straße 34	Stuttgart	1.98
2	2009-02-01 00:00:00	Barbarossastraße 19	Berlin	1.98
3	2009-02-01 00:00:00	8, Rue Hanovre	Paris	1.98
4	2009-03-04 00:00:00	1 Microsoft Way	Redmond	1.98
5	2009-03-04 00:00:00	1 Infinite Loop	Cupertino	1.98
6	2009-04-04 00:00:00	421 Bourke Street	Sidney	1.98
7	2009-04-04 00:00:00	Calle Lira, 198	Santiago	1.98
8	2009-05-05 00:00:00	Rua a Assunção 53	Lisbon	1.98
9	2009-05-05 00:00:00	Tauentzienstraße 8	Berlin	1.98
10	2009-06-05 00:00:00	Qe 7 Bloco G	Brasília	1.98
...	111 rows returned in 7ms			

The WHERE clause always comes *after* the FROM but *before* the ORDER BY. In the example above, the WHERE clause is added to return all invoices that are equal to 1.98. The = sign is referred to as a comparison operator.

ON YOUR OWN:

Using comparison operators, try out the following queries:

» Write a query that returns all invoices that are greater than 1.98.
» Write a query that returns all invoices that are greater than or equal to 1.98.
» Write a query that returns all invoices that are not 1.98.

Logical operators are also very useful. They can help you write more complex and specific queries that would be harder to accomplish with comparison operators. Let's say you were asked to find out how many invoices existed inside a certain range, such as between $1.98 and $5.00.

A good way to accomplish this is with the BETWEEN operator. The BETWEEN operator returns a range of values. The AND operator is used in conjunction with the BETWEEN operator to span the range of values we want to see in our result set. Our example below returns the range of invoices that fall between 1.98 and 5.00.

```
SELECT
    InvoiceDate,
    BillingAddress,
    BillingCity,
    Total
FROM
    invoices
WHERE
    Total BETWEEN 1.98 AND 5.00
ORDER BY
    InvoiceDate
```

As we can see with the first ten results of this query (Figure 46), the invoice totals we returned in our dataset are all between $1.98 and $5.00. The BETWEEN operator is inclusive of the parameters you give it. In other words, in the prior example, it would include any values that equaled 1.98 and 5.00. Using comparison operators, you could write `Total >= 1.98 AND Total <= 5.00` in your WHERE statement to achieve the same effect, but BETWEEN would be simpler.

NOTE

Although we are using the AND operator with BETWEEN in the preceding example, the AND operator has a much more extensive role as a logical operator and will be covered later in this chapter.

fig. 46

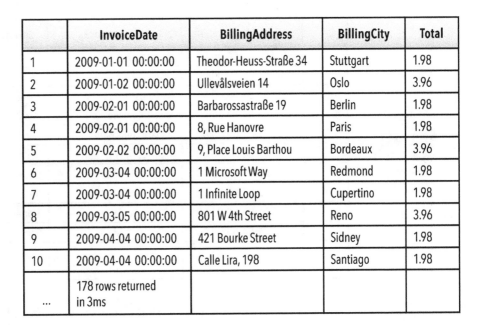

	InvoiceDate	BillingAddress	BillingCity	Total
1	2009-01-01 00:00:00	Theodor-Heuss-Straße 34	Stuttgart	1.98
2	2009-01-02 00:00:00	Ullevålsveien 14	Oslo	3.96
3	2009-02-01 00:00:00	Barbarossastraße 19	Berlin	1.98
4	2009-02-01 00:00:00	8, Rue Hanovre	Paris	1.98
5	2009-02-02 00:00:00	9, Place Louis Barthou	Bordeaux	3.96
6	2009-03-04 00:00:00	1 Microsoft Way	Redmond	1.98
7	2009-03-04 00:00:00	1 Infinite Loop	Cupertino	1.98
8	2009-03-05 00:00:00	801 W 4th Street	Reno	3.96
9	2009-04-04 00:00:00	421 Bourke Street	Sidney	1.98
10	2009-04-04 00:00:00	Calle Lira, 198	Santiago	1.98
...	178 rows returned in 3ms			

ON YOUR OWN:

» Order the previous query by the `Total` field. What is the highest invoice amount in this dataset?

Yet another useful operator is the `IN` operator, which is used to find a list of precise values. In our previous example, the `BETWEEN` operator returned every value in our *invoices* table that fell between 1.98 and 5.00. The `IN` operator allows us to find specific values within a dataset. The values are separated by a comma and wrapped in parentheses. This query returns only the invoice amounts that are exactly $1.98 or $3.96 (Figure 47).

```
SELECT
    InvoiceDate,
    BillingAddress,
    BillingCity,
    Total
FROM
    invoices
WHERE
    Total IN (1.98, 3.96)
ORDER BY
    InvoiceDate
```

	InvoiceDate	BillingAddress	BillingCity	Total
1	2009-01-01 00:00:00	Theodor-Heuss-Straße 34	Stuttgart	1.98
2	2009-01-02 00:00:00	Ullevålsveien 14	Oslo	3.96
3	2009-02-01 00:00:00	Barbarossastraße 19	Berlin	1.98
4	2009-02-01 00:00:00	8, Rue Hanovre	Paris	1.98
5	2009-02-02 00:00:00	9, Place Louis Barthou	Bordeaux	3.96
6	2009-03-04 00:00:00	1 Microsoft Way	Redmond	1.98
7	2009-03-04 00:00:00	1 Infinite Loop	Cupertino	1.98
8	2009-03-05 00:00:00	801 W 4th Street	Reno	3.96
9	2009-04-04 00:00:00	421 Bourke Street	Sidney	1.98
10	2009-04-04 00:00:00	Calle Lira, 198	Santiago	1.98
...	168 rows returned in 2ms			

GRAPHIC

fig. 47

NOTE

With the = operator, we can find only one value. With the IN operator, we can add as many values, separated by commas, as we need. We can also use the IN operator with text, as we will see in the following section.

ON YOUR OWN:
» How many records does the query above return?
» Write a query that lists all invoices that are $13.86, $18.86, and $21.86.

Filtering Records by Text

We can also use operators to return specific text, in a way similar to what we have done with numbers. Let's look at an example with comparison operators. We will answer the question: How many invoices were billed to Tucson?

To answer this question, we will structure our SELECT statement like we did for invoice totals, except this time we will focus on the billing city in our WHERE clause. The following query returns all invoices that have been billed in the city of Tucson:

```
SELECT
    InvoiceDate,
    BillingAddress,
    BillingCity,
    Total
```

```
FROM
    invoices
WHERE
    BillingCity = 'Tucson'
ORDER BY
    Total
```

	InvoiceDate	BillingAddress	BillingCity	Total
1	2012-03-011 00:00:00	1033 N Park Ave	Tucson	0.99
2	2011-01-15 00:00:00	1033 N Park Ave	Tucson	1.98
3	2013-09-02 00:00:00	1033 N Park Ave	Tucson	1.98
4	2011-04-19 00:00:00	1033 N Park Ave	Tucson	3.96
5	2011-07-22 00:00:00	1033 N Park Ave	Tucson	5.94
6	2009-06-10 00:00:00	1033 N Park Ave	Tucson	8.91
7	2013-10-13 00:00:00	1033 N Park Ave	Tucson	13.86
	7 rows returned in 1ms			

GRAPHIC

fig. 48

In this result set, we see that we have only seven invoices from Tucson.

NOTE

When using text as criteria in the WHERE clause, the text value(s) we specify must be surrounded by single quotes (BillingCity = 'Tucson').

REMEMBER

We are using = in the preceding example because we are looking for one value. If we wanted to search for multiple cities, we could use the IN operator similar to how we used it to retrieve numerical values.

```
SELECT
    InvoiceDate,
    BillingAddress,
    BillingCity,
    Total
FROM
    invoices
WHERE
    BillingCity IN ('Tucson', 'Paris', 'London')
ORDER BY
    Total
```

GRAPHIC

fig. 49

	InvoiceDate	BillingAddress	BillingCity	Total
1	2011-11-08 00:00:00	202 Hoxton Street	London	0.99
2	2012-03-11 00:00:00	1033 N Park Ave	Tucson	0.99
3	2012-08-13 00:00:00	8, Rue Hanovre	Paris	0.99
4	2013-01-15 00:00:00	113 Lupus St	London	0.99
5	2009-02-01 00:00:00	8, Rue Hanovre	Paris	1.98
6	2009-07-06 00:00:00	113 Lupus St	London	1.98
7	2010-04-11 00:00:00	4, Rue Milton	Paris	1.98
8	2010-09-13 00:00:00	202 Hoxton Street	London	1.98
9	2011-01-15 00:00:00	1033 N Park Ave	Tucson	1.98
10	2011-11-21 00:00:00	113 Lupus St	London	1.98
...	35 rows returned in 7ms			

Using the **LIKE** Operator to Search for Wildcards

In previous examples, we have used the = operator to search for exactly the text we are looking for. SQL also allows us to search for parts of a text value using the LIKE operator. This is particularly useful when we are not certain how a text value is spelled in a database. Also, there may be cases where a text value is not spelled correctly in our database. If we were to look for all invoices that were billed in cities that start with *T,* the criteria in our WHERE clause would need to be changed to accommodate this type of search.

What makes the LIKE operator so useful is its use of wildcard characters, which are represented by "%," also called the percent symbol. What follows the = sign is the only value you can expect to see in your result set. With the LIKE and wildcard, you can find variations on your input.

NOTE

Wildcard characters will always be enclosed in single quotation marks. Without quotation marks, % is an arithmetic operator known as modulo, as shown earlier in this chapter in the table of operators. Text searches are not case-sensitive. A lowercase *t* and an uppercase *T* will return the same results.

A wildcard symbol represents any number of any type of characters. As used in the example below, the query will search for any invoices that were billed in cities that start with *T.* Our results show that both Toronto and Tucson are now included.

```
SELECT
        InvoiceDate,
        BillingAddress,
        BillingCity,
        Total
FROM
        invoices
WHERE
        BillingCity LIKE 'T%'
ORDER BY
        Total
```

fig. 50

	InvoiceDate	BillingAddress	BillingCity	Total
1	2009-07-24 00:00:00	796 Dundas Street West	Toronto	0.99
2	2012-03-11 00:00:00	1033 N Park Ave	Tucson	0.99
3	2011-01-15 00:00:00	1033 N Park Ave	Tucson	1.98
4	2011-01-15 00:00:00	796 Dundas Street West	Toronto	1.98
5	2013-06-01 00:00:00	796 Dundas Street West	Toronto	1.98
6	2013-09-02 00:00:00	1033 N Park Ave	Tucson	1.98
7	2011-04-19 00:00:00	1033 N Park Ave	Tucson	3.96
8	2013-09-03 00:00:00	796 Dundas Street West	Toronto	3.96
9	2011-07-22 00:00:00	1033 N Park Ave	Tucson	5.94
10	2013-12-06 00:00:00	796 Dundas Street West	Toronto	5.94
...	14 rows returned in 1ms			

Adding another percent symbol before the *T* would change the search to any invoice whose billing city has a *T* anywhere in it.

```
SELECT
    InvoiceDate,
    BillingAddress,
    BillingCity,
    Total
FROM
    invoices
WHERE
    BillingCity LIKE '%T%'
ORDER BY
    Total
```

	InvoiceDate	BillingAddress	BillingCity	Total
1	2009-01-19 00:00:00	Berger Straße 10	Frankfurt	0.99
2	2009-02-19 00:00:00	1600 Amphitheatre Parkway	Mountain View	0.99
3	2009-07-24 00:00:00	796 Dundas Street West	Toronto	0.99
4	2010-08-31 00:00:00	Celsiusg. 9	Stockholm	0.99
5	2010-10-01 00:00:00	230 Elgin Street	Ottawa	0.99
6	2011-01-02 00:00:00	2211 W Berry Street	Fort Worth	0.99
7	2011-09-07 00:00:00	Rua dos Campeões Europeus de Viena, 4350	Porto	0.99
...	126 rows returned in 2ms			

NOTE

This of course does not exclude cities that begin or end with lowercase *t*. The % can represent any letter(s) at all, including *t*.

The LIKE operator can also be used to exclude results that match specified criteria. By placing the NOT keyword in front of LIKE, you can exclude records from your query result.

```
SELECT
    InvoiceDate,
    BillingAddress,
    BillingCity,
    Total
FROM
    invoices
WHERE
    BillingCity NOT LIKE '%T%'
ORDER BY
    Total
```

	InvoiceDate	BillingAddress	BillingCity	Total
1	2009-03-22 00:00:00	110 Raeburn Pl	Edinburgh	0.99
2	2009-04-22 00:00:00	5112 48 Street	Yellowknife	0.99
3	2009-05-23 00:00:00	Praça Pio X, 119	Rio de Janeiro	0.99
4	2009-06-23 00:00:00	C/ San Bernardo 85	Madrid	0.99
5	2009-08-24 00:00:00	Grétrystraat 63	Brussels	0.99
6	2009-09-24 00:00:00	3 Chatham Street	Dublin	0.99
7	2009-10-25 00:00:00	319 N. Frances Street	Madison	0.99
8	2009-11-25 00:00:00	Ullevålsveien 14	Oslo	0.99
9	2009-12-26 00:00:00	9, Place Louis Barthou	Bordeaux	0.99
10	2010-01-26 00:00:00	801 W 4th Street	Reno	0.99
...	286 rows returned in 4ms			

We can see from these examples that there are many helpful ways to use the wildcard operator. Here are a few of the most common:

GRAPHIC

fig. 53

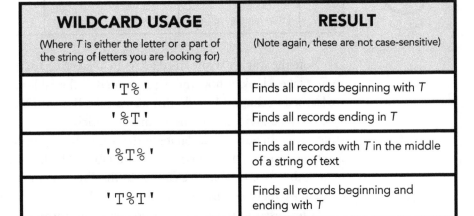

WILDCARD USAGE (Where *T* is either the letter or a part of the string of letters you are looking for)	RESULT (Note again, these are not case-sensitive)
'T%'	Finds all records beginning with *T*
'%T'	Finds all records ending in *T*
'%T%'	Finds all records with *T* in the middle of a string of text
'T%T'	Finds all records beginning and ending with *T*

NOTE

A good way to think about the wildcard is to treat the % symbol as "whatever else." For example, when you specify '%T%' you are saying "I don't care what comes before or after, as long as there is a *T* somewhere in that string of text that isn't in the first or last position."

Filtering Records by Date

Taking what we learned about both numbers and text, we can also search for invoices on a specific date. Look at the following example:

```
SELECT
    InvoiceDate,
    BillingAddress,
    BillingCity,
    Total
FROM
    invoices
WHERE
    InvoiceDate = '2009-01-03 00:00:00'
ORDER BY
    Total
```

fig. 54

	InvoiceDate	BillingAddress	BillingCity	Total
1	2009-01-03 00:00:00	Grétrystraat 63	Brussels	5.94
	1 rows returned in 1ms			

Note the way we wrote the date. When querying for dates, it is important to first take a look at how the date is stored in the table you are querying. As we learned in chapter 1, to do this we visit the Browse Data tab and select the *invoices* table and observe the format in which the InvoiceDate column stores dates. In our sample database, dates are stored as yyyy-mm-dd 00:00:00. Next, let's go to the Database Structure tab and look at the InvoiceDate field of the *invoices* table. We can see in the Type column that this field stores dates in a data type called DATETIME.

When used in the WHERE clause, dates are surrounded by single quotes just as text is. When querying with dates, use the same operators used when querying with numbers: =, >, <, BETWEEN, etc.

ON YOUR OWN:

» Get all invoices that were issued between January 1, 2009, and December 31, 2009.

» Find the top 10 highest value invoices that occurred after July 5, 2009.

The DATE( ) Function

When working with dates in SQL, we have access to a number of functions that help us obtain more refined results by specifying parts of a date we are interested in. We saw in our previous example that the InvoiceDate column of the *invoices* table is defined as a DATETIME data type. Therefore, when we were specifying a date value in our WHERE clause, we needed to include the time portion of it (2009-01-03 00:00:00). The DATE() function allows us to exclude the time when specifying our date criteria.

```
SELECT
    InvoiceDate,
    BillingAddress,
    BillingCity,
    Total
FROM
    invoices
```

```
WHERE
    DATE(InvoiceDate) = '2009-01-03'
ORDER BY
    Total
```

fig. 55

	InvoiceDate	BillingAddress	BillingCity	Total
1	2009-01-03 00:00:00	Grétrystraat 63	Brussels	5.94
	1 rows returned in 2ms			

The result of this query is identical to that of the query before it. However, using the DATE() function saves us a bit of time in typing our query when the time information is either blank or not relevant.

There are many functions available in SQL. The DATE() function is particularly useful when using the WHERE clause to sort records by date. In chapter 7, we will explore using other functions in our queries in a more comprehensive way.

Using the AND and OR Operators with Two Separate Fields

So far in this chapter, we have only used operators to select a subset of one field. For example, we have used the AND operator with the BETWEEN operator to filter results from the Total field between two different numerical values. We can also use the AND and OR operators to specify criteria from multiple fields. The query below uses the AND together with the DATE function to find all invoices after 2010-01-02 with a total of less than $3.00. The result of this query must satisfy both conditions: (DATE(InvoiceDate) > '2010-01-02' AND Total < 3).

```
SELECT
    InvoiceDate,
    BillingAddress,
    BillingCity,
    Total
FROM
    invoices
```

```
WHERE
    DATE(InvoiceDate) > '2010-01-02' AND Total < 3
ORDER BY
    Total
```

GRAPHIC

fig. 56

	InvoiceDate	BillingAddress	BillingCity	Total
1	2010-01-26 00:00:00	801 W 4th Street	Reno	0.99
2	2010-03-29 00:00:00	Barbarossastraße 19	Berlin	0.99
3	2010-04-29 00:00:00	1 Microsoft Way	Redmond	0.99
4	2010-05-30 00:00:00	421 Bourke Street	Sidney	0.99
5	2010-06-30 00:00:00	Rua da Assunção 53	Lisbon	0.99
6	2010-07-31 00:00:00	Qe 7 Bloco G	Brasília	0.99
7	2010-08-31 00:00:00	Celsiusg. 9	Stockholm	0.99
8	2010-10-01 00:00:00	230 Elgin Street	Ottawa	0.99
9	2010-11-01 00:00:00	Sønder Boulevard 51	Copenhage	0.99
10	2010-12-02 00:00:00	Via Degli Scipioni, 43	Rome	0.99
...	136 rows returned in 3ms			

We can see from our results that only invoices after the second of January 2010, whose total is under $3.00, are returned.

NOTE

You can add additional AND operators to search for additional criteria. As with the IN operator, you are not limited to only two values.

ON YOUR OWN:
» Find all invoices whose billing city starts with *P* and whose total is greater than $2.00.

The OR Operator
The OR operator allows you to find the records that match *any* of the criteria you ask for. The following query searches for all invoices whose billing city starts with *P* or starts with *D*.

```
SELECT
    InvoiceDate,
    BillingAddress,
    BillingCity,
    Total
FROM
    invoices
WHERE
    BillingCity LIKE 'p%' OR BillingCity LIKE 'd%'
ORDER BY
    Total
```

	InvoiceDate	BillingAddress	BillingCity	Total
1	2009-09-24 00:00:00	3 Chatham Street	Dublin	0.99
2	2011-02-02 00:00:00	Klanova 9/506	Prague	0.99
3	2011-03-05 00:00:00	68, Rue Jouvence	Dijon	0.99
4	2011-09-07 00:00:00	Rua dos Campeões Europeus de Viena, 4350	Porto	0.99
5	2012-04-11 00:00:00	Rilská 3174/6	Prague	0.99
6	2012-08-13 00:00:00	8, Rue Hanovre	Paris	0.99
7	2009-02-01 00:00:00	8, Rue Hanovre	Paris	1.98
8	2009-12-08 00:00:00	Klanova 9/506	Prague	1.98
9	2010-01-08 00:00:00	68, Rue Jouvence	Dijon	1.98
10	2010-04-11 00:00:00	4, Rue Milton	Paris	1.98
...	56 rows returned in 4ms			

GRAPHIC

fig. 57

Using Parentheses with AND and OR to Specify the Order of Operations

When writing longer WHERE clauses that include multiple logical operators, SQL follows an order of operations similar to what is used for basic arithmetic. You may have heard of the acronym PEMDAS (parentheses, exponents, multiplication/division, addition/subtraction) if you live in the United States or BEMDAS (brackets, exponents, etc.) if you live in a country more influenced by the United Kingdom. If you have not heard of either, don't worry. We have a simple way of handling the order of operations, but for now, let's look at how a statement functions with both an AND operator and an OR operator. Let's say we wanted to look at all the invoices over $1.98 from any cities whose names start with *P* or *D*. We could write the following:

```
SELECT
  InvoiceDate,
  BillingAddress,
  BillingCity,
  Total
FROM
  invoices
WHERE
  Total > 1.98 AND BillingCity LIKE 'p%' OR
  BillingCity LIKE 'd%'
ORDER BY
  Total
```

GRAPHIC

fig. 58

	InvoiceDate	BillingAddress	BillingCity	Total
1	2009-09-24 00:00:00	3 Chatham Street	Dublin	0.99
2	2011-03-05 00:00:00	68, Rue Jouvence	Dijon	0.99
3	2010-01-08 00:00:00	68, Rue Jouvence	Dijon	1.98
4	2010-06-12 00:00:00	12, Community Centre	Delhi	1.98
5	2011-03-18 00:00:00	3 Chatham Street	Dublin	1.98
6	2012-08-26 00:00:00	68, Rue Jouvence	Dijon	1.98
7	2012-10-27 00:00:00	12, Community Centre	Delhi	1.98
8	2013-08-02 00:00:00	3 Chatham Street	Dublin	1.98
9	2011-06-06 00:00:00	4, Rue Milton	Paris	1.99
10	2010-12-02 00:00:00	12, Community Centre	Delhi	1.99
...	43 rows returned in 2ms			

There is a slight problem with this query as written. When the query is executed, the SQL browser combines the two conditions immediately on either side of the AND operator first, returning results for invoices whose total is greater than $1.98 *and* whose billing cities begin with *P*, then it processes the condition to the right of the OR operator completely separately, as if the AND did not exist. In other words, it first looks for the results where Total > 1.98 AND BillingCity LIKE 'p%', then it looks for all results where BillingCity LIKE 'd%', then it returns the results for both in ascending order by Total.

If you have typed the above query into your SQL browser, you will notice that there are results for less than $1.98, but only for cities starting with *D*.

That is because, in the SQL order of operations, the AND operator is processed first and the OR is processed second. This result isn't exactly what we originally wanted, but there is an easy way to ensure that the SQL browser processes our query the way we intended, without our having to resort to a logic table.

NOTE

SQL processes the AND operator like multiplication and the OR operator like addition, unless you include parentheses. Without parentheses, the AND will be processed in the same way that 3*2+1 would equal 7, but 3*(2+1) would equal 9.

When parentheses are added as shown in the example below, the SQL browser first looks for all the records that satisfy the criteria between the parentheses: (BillingCity LIKE 'p%' OR BillingCity LIKE 'd%'). Then, from within only these records, it looks for records where the total is greater than $1.98 (Total > 1.98).

```
SELECT
    InvoiceDate,
    BillingAddress,
    BillingCity,
    Total
FROM
    invoices
WHERE
    Total > 1.98 AND (BillingCity LIKE 'p%' OR
    BillingCity LIKE 'd%')
ORDER BY
    Total
```

fig. 59

	InvoiceDate	BillingAddress	BillingCity	Total
1	2011-06-06 00:00:00	4, Rue Milton	Paris	1.99
2	2013-12-22 00:00:00	12, Community Centre	Dehli	1.99
3	2011-06-19 00:00:00	8, Rue Hanovre	Paris	2.98
4	2010-03-12 00:00:00	Klanova 9/506	Prague	3.96
5	2010-04-12 00:00:00	68, Rue Jouvence	Dijon	3.96
6	2010-07-14 00:00:00	4, Rue Milton	Paris	3.96
7	2010-10-15 00:00:00	Rua dos Campeões Europeus de Viena, 4350	Porto	3.96
8	2011-05-20 00:00:00	Rilská 3174/6	Prague	3.96
9	2011-09-21 00:00:00	8, Rue Hanovre	Paris	3.96
10	2013-01-29 00:00:00	12, Community Centre	Delhi	3.96
...	35 rows returned in 1ms			

Writing the query this way ensures that all invoice totals greater than $1.98 are returned from either *P* cities or *D* cities, which was what we initially wanted.

Although it is good to know how SQL processes logical operators, it is better to just use parentheses whenever you are using multiple operators so that it is clear to you, and anyone else who reads your code, what you actually intended. If you would like more practice, try the following exercises both with and without parentheses to see how it affects the result.

ON YOUR OWN:

» Run the query again and observe if there are any values in the Total column that are less than $1.98.
» Find all invoices that have total values higher than $3.00 whose billing city starts with *P* or *D*.

The CASE Statement

The CASE statement allows you to create a new, temporary field in your database that serves as a label for your data based on unique user-specified conditions. To better understand the utility of the CASE statement, consider the following scenario from our fictional company, sTunes.

Operational Scenario

The sTunes sales team has a new sales goal. They want as many sTunes customers as possible to spend between seven and fifteen dollars when purchasing music from the sTunes online store. Thus, they have created the following categories: *Baseline Purchase, Low Purchase, Target Purchase,* and *Top Performer*.

Since the cost of a song varies between $0.99 and $1.99, any invoice total in this range is considered a *Baseline Purchase*. Invoice totals between $2.00 and $6.99 are labeled *Low Purchase*. Since the target sales goal is between $7.00 and $15.00, any sales in this category are labeled *Target Purchase*. Any sale above $15.00 is seen as a *Top Performer*.

Based on these categories, the sTunes sales department wants to see if any information can be gleaned from the database concerning the sales in all of the listed categories.

We can use a CASE statement to create a new field in our *invoices* table called `PurchaseType`. This will appear alongside the other preexisting fields in our query as if it was just another field in the database.

Adding the CASE Statement to a Query

To add the CASE statement to our query, we must start with a SELECT statement with the preexisting fields we are interested in from the *invoices* table. First, we create a simple SELECT statement similar to the type we have used since chapter 4.

```
SELECT
    InvoiceDate,
    BillingAddress,
    BillingCity,
    Total
FROM
    invoices
ORDER BY
    BillingCity
```

For this first example, we are going to order our results by billing city so we can see our sales goals by geographic region.

To add our CASE statement to this query, we place it at the bottom of the SELECT portion of our query after all the existing fields. We start by adding the keyword CASE, followed by the keyword END. Between these two keywords we start testing for conditions. Each test begins with the keyword WHEN, followed by a logical test, which is similar to what you would add in a WHERE clause. Our first case to test is *Baseline Purchases*, which is any invoice under $2.00, in other words "TOTAL < 2.00". After the logical condition, we then specify what we want to happen if that condition is met. This is done with the THEN keyword. The label we desire for cases under $2.00 is 'Baseline Purchase' which is what is specified for our operational scenario.

This same sequence can be repeated for as many conditions as we want to test. So we repeat this process for the rest of the sales categories mentioned in our operational scenario. The ELSE keyword always follows the last explicit condition listed. Any records that have yet to be categorized will take their assignment from the category named in the ELSE clause.

The ELSE keyword doesn't need to be included, but it is good practice to include it. There may be outliers in your data that fall outside of your conditions. The ELSE clause will capture these outliers and you can figure out what to do with them. If you do not include an ELSE clause, any results in your dataset that fall outside of your conditions will be returned as NULL.

The last thing we do is create an alias that will become the name of the new field in our database. This alias will go after our END statement. We will call our new field PurchaseType.

We create aliases using the AS keyword. So our CASE statement terminates with END AS and then the alias name we chose for the new field in our table.

Putting this all together gives us the following (Figure 60):

```
SELECT
    InvoiceDate,
    BillingAddress,
    BillingCity,
    Total,
    CASE
    WHEN TOTAL < 2.00 THEN 'Baseline Purchase'
    WHEN TOTAL BETWEEN 2.00 AND 6.99 THEN 'Low
    Purchase'
    WHEN TOTAL BETWEEN 7.00 AND 15.00 THEN 'Target
    Purchase'
    ELSE 'Top Performers'
    END AS PurchaseType
FROM
    invoices
ORDER BY
    BillingCity
```

If we scroll over a bit in our results, we can see that the SQL browser added a new category called PurchaseType and added all our sales goal categories to the data.

We can see in the result set that all the categories we tested for are represented according to their respective price brackets (PurchaseType).

	InvoiceDate	BillingAddress	BillingCity	Total	PurchaseType
1	2009-05-10 00:00:00	Lijnbaansgracht 120bg	Amsterdam	8.91	Target Purchase
2	2010-12-15 00:00:00	Lijnbaansgracht 120bg	Amsterdam	1.91	Baseline Purchase
3	2011-03-19 00:00:00	Lijnbaansgracht 120bg	Amsterdam	3.96	Low Purchase
4	2011-06-21 00:00:00	Lijnbaansgracht 120bg	Amsterdam	8.94	Target Purchase
5	2012-02-09 00:00:00	Lijnbaansgracht 120bg	Amsterdam	0.99	Baseline Purchase
6	2013-08-02 00:00:00	Lijnbaansgracht 120bg	Amsterdam	1.98	Baseline Purchase
7	2013-09-12 00:00:00	Lijnbaansgracht 120bg	Amsterdam	13.86	Target Purchase
8	2009-04-05 00:00:00	3,Raj Bhavan Road	Bangalore	3.96	Low Purchase
9	2009-07-08 00:00:00	3,Raj Bhavan Road	Bangalore	5.94	Low Purchase
10	2010-02-26 00:00:00	3,Raj Bhavan Road	Bangalore	1.99	Baseline Purchase
...	412 rows returned in 17ms				

GRAPHIC

fig. 60

NOTE

Using the ORDER BY clause, we can also order our results by the new field we created, which would show each category of purchase type alphabetically, starting with "Baseline Purchase" and ending with "Top Performers." We conveniently named these categories to be consistent with increasing purchase price for clarity, but they can be named anything you want them to be.

Now that we have created new categories for our data, there are a lot of useful ways we can manipulate the rest of the SELECT statement to learn more about the demographics of our customers based on our new sales categories.

Our case statement is written, so we can answer some pertinent questions, including the following:

» What cities do our top-performing sales come from?

» Are our top-performing sales mainly from the United States or from other parts of the world?

» From what cities are the most baseline purchases made?

Let's take a closer look at the first question. We can modify our existing query with a WHERE clause in order to look only at top performers and order them by city.

```
SELECT
    InvoiceDate,
    BillingAddress,
    BillingCity,
    Total,
    CASE
    WHEN TOTAL < 2.00 THEN 'Baseline Purchase'
    WHEN TOTAL BETWEEN 2.00 AND 6.99 THEN 'Low
    Purchase'
    WHEN TOTAL BETWEEN 7.00 AND 15.00 THEN 'Target
    Purchase'
    ELSE 'Top Performers'
    END AS PurchaseType
FROM
    invoices
WHERE PurchaseType = 'Top Performers'
ORDER BY
    BillingCity
```

GRAPHIC

fig. 61

	InvoiceDate	BillingAddress	BillingCity	Total	PurchaseType
1	2010-02-18 00:00:00	Erzsébet krt. 58.	Budapest	21.86	Top Performers
2	2010-03-21 00:00:00	162 E Superior Street	Chicago	15.86	Top Performers
3	2012-10-06 00:00:00	68, Rue Jouvence	Dijon	16.86	Top Performers
4	2011-04-28 00:00:00	3 Chatham Street	Dublin	21.86	Top Performers
5	2012-08-05 00:00:00	2211 W Berry Street	Fort Worth	23.86	Top Performers
6	2011-05-29 00:00:00	319 N. Frances Street	Madison	18.86	Top Performers
7	2011-06-29 00:00:00	Ullevålsveien 14	Oslo	15.86	Top Performers
8	2012-09-05 00:00:00	Klanova 9/506	Prague	16.9	Top Performers
9	2013-11-13 00:00:00	Rilská 3174/6	Prague	25.9	Top Performers
10	2010-01-13 00:00:00	Calle Lira, 198	Santiago	17.9	Top Performers
...	11 rows returned in 6ms				

Looking at the result of this query, we can determine that our top performers come mainly from outside of the US.

The combinations of fields we can search for or narrow down to is virtually limitless. For example, we could also organize the data by invoice date to see if there are any seasonal purchase trends. Using CASE statements, along with the WHERE clause and the operators we learned about in this chapter, can really help us turn our data into information that would be of direct interest to our sales team.

NOTE

In our examples in this chapter, we have always used the CASE statement in the SELECT portion of our query after we have listed the fields we want to display. In your upcoming real-life SQL adventures, you may also encounter a query with a CASE statement contained in a WHERE clause, however uncommon. All that is important for now is to remember that a CASE statement must be defined in SELECT but can be referenced elsewhere.

Data Analysis Checkpoint

1. Create a query for the *invoices* table that includes a CASE statement that labels all sales from billing country USA as "Domestic Sales" and all other sales as "Foreign Sales." Label your new field as SalesType after your END AS statement.

2. Order this data by the new field SalesType.

3. How many invoices from Domestic Sales were over $15?

3

1. SELECT
        Billing Country,
        Total,
        CASE
        WHEN Billing Country = 'USA' THEN 'Domestic Sales'
        ELSE 'Foreign Sales'
        END AS SalesType

   FROM
        invoices

   ORDER BY
        SalesType

   WHERE
        SalesType = 'Domestic Sales' AND
                                Total ⅃ 15

Chapter Recap

» Operators are special SQL keywords that are used with SQL clauses to filter data by specific conditions.

» Using the WHERE clause with a combination of different operators can enable the user to search records for specific text, dates, and numbers.

» The DATE() function allows us to exclude the timecode when specifying our date criteria.

» The order of operations when using logical operators (such as AND/OR) is controlled by parentheses ().

» The CASE statement allows you to label records with a special field name based on user-specified logical conditions.

| 6 |
Working with Multiple Tables

In all the queries we have written so far, we have only looked at retrieving data from one table (at a time). Although we have learned some powerful querying methods, nothing in our growing SQL tool kit really harnesses the power of a relational database. Our sTunes database has thirteen tables. Each table contains some, but not all, of the information about our fictional company. In order to answer more complex questions from our sTunes company management, we will need to access data from multiple tables simultaneously. This chapter will help you become comfortable obtaining data from two or more tables with a single query by using powerful tools called joins.

What Are Joins?

A join is a command that combines the fields from two or more tables of a relational database. Let's take a look at a very simple example using the *invoices* table in our sTunes database. We have worked with the *invoices* table extensively in previous chapters, so by now we should be very familiar with the fields in this particular table. As we can see from the Browse Data tab of the SQL browser (Figure 62), the *invoices* table has nine fields. Each invoice has an identification number known as InvoiceId. Each customer (that has generated an invoice) has an identification number known as CustomerId. The *invoices* table also has fields for the invoice date and invoice total. The rest of the fields in this table are dedicated to the invoice billing address.

fig. 62

fig. 63

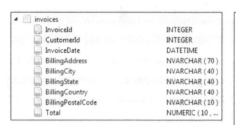

Let's say our sTunes marketing department wants to get to know the customer base better. They ask us for a full list of customer names (first and last) next to all the invoices generated by that customer. How could we write such a query using only the *invoices* table? We would not be able to answer this question in one query using the skills we have learned so far. Our *invoices* table does not contain the names of our customers. Instead, the *invoices* table contains a field called `CustomerId`. To discover how to display a list of invoices that includes the customers who generated those invoices, we need to look at the *invoices* and *customers* tables side by side.

If we look at the *customers* table in Figure 63, we can see that this table contains the information we want: the first and last names of all our sTunes customers. This table also has a `CustomerId` field. If we look closely at the icons in the *customers* table, we can see that this version of the `CustomerId` field has a small key icon next to it. We learned in chapter 1 that this key icon is the symbol for a primary key, the unique identifying field for that particular table.

Every table should have at least one field that serves as a primary key. A primary key in one table often exists as a foreign key in a different table.

Since `CustomerId` is the primary key of the *customers* table, and there is a similar field of the same name in the *invoices* table, these two `CustomerId` fields provide us with the link we need to access both of these tables simultaneously. We now have all the information required to join these two tables together and produce a list of invoices with customer names.

A `JOIN` clause merging both of these tables together would look like this:

```
SELECT
    *
FROM
    invoices
INNER JOIN
    customers
ON
    invoices.CustomerId = customers.CustomerId
```

In this example, we are using a join called an `INNER JOIN`. Several different types of joins will be introduced in this chapter. Each join functions in a slightly different way. We will address those differences later. At this point, all we really need to know is that joins allow us to access fields from different tables.

When we look at this query, there is a lot we already know. The query begins with `SELECT`, as all our queries have so far. We use the * symbol in this example, which we learned about in chapter 4, to return all the fields in a table. We are selecting all fields from the *invoices* table and joining them to all the fields in the *customers* table. We use the `ON` keyword to provide the query with the link between these two tables, which is the `CustomerId` field. Since there are two versions of the `CustomerId` field (one in each table), we must use special notation (in the form of `tablename.FieldName`) to tell the SQL browser which specific version to use. We set the `CustomerId` field from the *invoices* table (written as `invoices.CustomerId`) equal to the `CustomerId` field from the *customers* table (written as `customers.CustomerId`). When we run the query, the resulting output is shown in Figure 64.

By using the * symbol, we have combined the nine fields of the *invoices* table with the thirteen fields of the *customers* table for a total of twenty-two fields. We have truncated some of these fields for print, but we can view all twenty-two fields in DB Browser by using the horizontal scroll bar in the Results Pane of our Execute SQL tab.

GRAPHIC

fig. 64

	InvoiceId	CustomerId	...	Total	CustomerId	FirstName	LastName	...	SupportRepId
1	98	1	...	3.98	1	Luís	Gonçalves	...	3
2	121	1	...	3.96	1	Luís	Gonçalves	...	3
3	143	1	...	5.94	1	Luís	Gonçalves	...	3
4	195	1	...	.99	1	Luís	Gonçalves	...	3
5	316	1	...	1.98	1	Luís	Gonçalves	...	3
6	327	1	...	13.86	1	Luís	Gonçalves	...	3
7	382	1	...	8.91	1	Luís	Gonçalves	...	3
8	1	2	...	1.98	2	Leonie	Köhler	...	5
9	12	2	...	13.86	2	Leonie	Köhler	...	5
10	67	2	...	8.91	2	Leonie	Köhler	...	5
...	412 rows returned in 17ms				...				

How Joins Interact with Relational Database Structure

There are a few things we can observe now that we have combined the *invoices* table with the *customers* table. If we look at the InvoiceId field from the invoices section of the result set (Figure 64), we can see that the first seven records are linked to the same CustomerId. This link tells us that customer number 1 is responsible for generating all seven of those invoices. If we follow along to the customers table portion of the result set, we can see that this customer's name is Luís Gonçalves. One customer is linked to many invoices. In the language of a relational database (introduced in chapter 1), we can say that the *customers* table has a one-to-many relationship with the *invoices* table. It makes sense that a single customer, with a single CustomerId, could generate many invoices (by ordering multiple songs) but he would retain the same CustomerId number in the *invoices* table. Another way of describing this relationship is to organize the database schema using an entity relationship diagram (ERD).

Looking at Figure 65, we can see a graphical representation of the relationship between the *customers* table and the *invoices* table. If we look at the rest of our database, we can see many other instances of primary and foreign keys establishing a relationship between different tables. Part of creating and using joins is understanding these relationships. In order to join tables together, we must be able to identify primary keys and foreign keys and understand which fields we want to select.

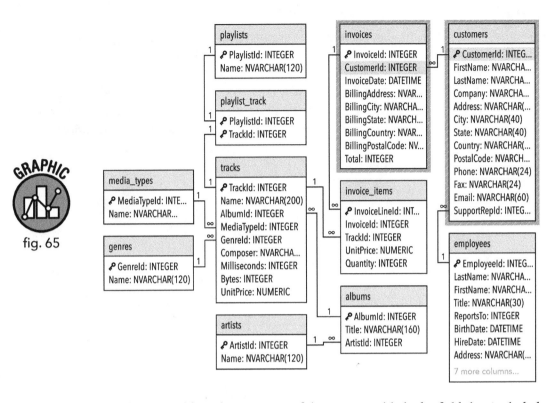

fig. 65

Joins would not be necessary if the *invoices* table had a field that included all the customer names. Going one step further, instead of a database with thirteen tables, we could have just one giant table that contained every field.

Q: Why are databases designed with multiple tables?

Answer: In a relational database, the process of distributing fields across related tables is known as **normalization**. Normalization keeps the sizes of databases smaller, as it reduces the need to have duplicate fields in the same table. The need to normalize databases increases as database size increases. Saving even a few seconds of query processing time is worth it. Considering the staggering size of some databases, every second counts. Imagine if your Google search took five minutes rather than a few seconds.

Now that we have identified the common link between the two related fields in both the *invoices* table and the *customers* table, we can take a closer look at how we write queries with joins.

Using Joins with an Alias

We have seen from our first example that joins have a special syntax when referring to field names. Since two tables in any given database may have fields with identical names, when creating joins it is necessary to specify the table name when listing a specific field so that the SQL browser knows exactly which version of that field we are referencing. This syntax requires that the table name be listed first, followed by a period, followed by the field name. Joins are often used with aliases to reduce the amount of typing required, as well as to increase readability. The following two joins are identical in function.

```
SELECT
    *
FROM
    invoices
INNER JOIN
    customers
ON
    invoices.CustomerId = customers.CustomerId
```

```
SELECT
    *
FROM
    invoices AS i
INNER JOIN
    customers AS c
ON
    i.CustomerId = c.CustomerId
```

NOTE

Aliases for joins are designed to be concise and readable by convention. These aliases are usually single letters, with the letter used being the first letter of the relevant table (`tablename.FieldName` would become `t.FieldName`). We will be using single-letter aliases for table names for the remainder of this chapter.

To further demonstrate the need for aliases when working with joins, let's go back to our original fictional scenario for this chapter. sTunes management wanted a list showing customer names and the invoices that each customer generated. When we wrote our first join in this chapter, we used the * symbol to select all the fields from each table. This query resulted in a massive twenty-two-field result set. But we were only interested in the customer names and invoice information. In addition to that, when we use the * symbol, we have no control over the order in which our fields are displayed. For example, let's say sTunes management specified that they wanted their customer list displayed with the last name first. To produce output with a customized order, we have to select individual field names in our SELECT statement instead of using the * symbol. Let's create a join similar to the ones above, but this time, let's specify in our query that we want to see the LastName and FirstName fields from the *customers* table and the InvoiceId, CustomerId, InvoiceDate, and Total from the *invoices* table. Because we are dealing with two tables that contain some fields with identical field names, when we list our individual fields in our SELECT statement we must use the same tablename. FieldName notation we have used in the ON clause of our joins—with one alteration: instead of listing the full table name, we will use an alias consisting of the first letter of the table, followed by a period, and then the field name. Finally, we want to order the results by the customer's last name. The resulting query would look like this:

```
SELECT
    c.LastName,
    c.FirstName,
    i.InvoiceId,
    i.CustomerId,
    i.InvoiceDate,
    i.Total
FROM
    invoices AS i
INNER JOIN
    customers AS c
ON
    i.CustomerId = c.CustomerId
ORDER BY
    c.LastName
```

fig. 66

	LastName	FirstName	InvoiceId	CustomerId	InvoiceDate	Total
1	Almeida	Roberto	34	12	2009-05-23 00:00:00	0.99
2	Almeida	Roberto	155	12	2010-11-14 00:00:00	1.98
3	Almeida	Roberto	166	12	2010-12-25 00:00:00	13.86
4	Almeida	Roberto	221	12	2011-08-25 00:00:00	8.91
5	Almeida	Roberto	350	12	2013-03-31 00:00:00	1.98
6	Almeida	Roberto	373	12	2013-07-03 00:00:00	3.96
7	Almeida	Roberto	395	12	2013-10-05 00:00:00	5.94
8	Barnett	Julia	71	28	2009-11-07 00:00:00	1.98
9	Barnett	Julia	82	28	2009-12-18 00:00:00	13.86
10	Barnett	Julia	137	28	2010-08-18 00:00:00	8.91
...	412 rows returned in 14ms					

Although it appears that we reference aliases (in the SELECT statement) *before* we define them (in the FROM and INNER JOIN statements), we must remember that the SQL browser does not process our queries in the exact way we humans would read them.

Looking at the first ten results of this query, we can see that listing specific fields in a specific order is much more manageable than returning all the fields with the * symbol. We can also imagine how much more complex this join would be if we had to type out the table name every time we referenced a field name.

In most cases it is a best practice to specify individual field names in your select statement and avoid using the * symbol. Throughout this chapter, however, we will only be using the * symbol for demonstrative purposes to explain JOIN structure.

Join Types and Their Differences

As we mentioned in the beginning of this chapter, there are several different types of joins. So far, we have used joins to give us access to the fields of multiple tables. We have identified the primary key of the *customers* table, identified a similar foreign key in the *invoices* table, and used the ON keyword to link the two tables together, hoping that all the data matches up.

Q: What happens if the data from the tables we join does not match up completely?

For example, what if a customer—let's call him Customer 6—deleted his sTunes account and was subsequently removed from the *customers* table? Because our sTunes company is required to keep financial records, there is still evidence from the *invoices* table that Customer 6 made a purchase at some point. It is not unusual to find discrepancies in databases, and we must decide whether we want our queries to include data that does not match up or to exclude it completely. To handle discrepancies between tables, different types of joins are used. To understand this concept, it is helpful to look at join types in the abstract using a slightly simplified version of our *invoices* and *customers* tables.

The following tables are a bit different from the ones in our sTunes database. We have kept the basic structure of both tables identical to sTunes *invoices* and *customers* tables but have reduced the tables to just five records each, eliminated some of the fields, simplified the record names, and added a few records in each table that differ from the records in the other table.

fig. 67

SIMPLIFIED INVOICES TABLE

InvoiceId	CustomerId	InvoiceDate	BillingAddress	Total
1	2	1/1/2018	Billing Address 2	$1.00
2	2	2/1/2018	Billing Address 2	$2.00
3	3	3/1/2018	Billing Address 3	$3.00
4	4	4/1/2018	Billing Address 4	$4.00
5	6	5/1/2017	Billing Address 6	$5.00

SIMPLIFIED CUSTOMERS TABLE

CustomerId	Name	Address
1	Customer 1	Address 1
2	Customer 2	Address 2
3	Customer 3	Address 3
4	Customer 4	Address 4
5	Customer 5	Address 6

As we look at our simplified *invoices* and *customers* tables, we can identify a few discrepancies. First, our *invoices* table shows that someone with a customer ID of 6 made a purchase on 5/1/2017, but this customer does not appear in our *customers* table. Also, it appears that Customer 1 and Customer 5 never made a purchase at all, since those customer ID numbers do not show up in the *invoices* table. Customer 2 shows up twice, so we can infer that that customer made two purchases. Since the records for Customer 1 and Customer 5 exist in the *customers* table but not the *invoices* table, and Customer 6 only exists in the *invoices* table, each table contains at least one unique record that does not exist in the other table. Now we can attempt to join these two tables together and observe how the output is handled depending on which type of join we use. Let's start with our familiar inner join.

The Inner Join

An inner join only returns matching records. Any unmatched data from either table is ignored. Joins are often described with Venn diagrams, as seen in Figure 68. An inner join represents only the overlapping section of the Venn diagram.

INNER JOIN

fig. 68

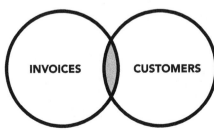

```
SELECT *
FROM invoices AS i
INNER JOIN customers AS c
ON i.CustomerId = c.CustomerId
```

In this example, our inner join will ignore Invoice 5 from our *invoices* table because this invoice refers to a customer (Customer 6) that does not appear on our *customers* table. Likewise, Customers 1 and 5 (from the *customers* table) did not generate any invoices, so that record is ignored as well. As the Venn diagram shows, only the overlapping data is included. Figure 69 is a visual representation of how an inner join is created from two tables with disparate data:

GRAPHIC

fig. 69

Simplified Invoices Table

InvoiceId	CustomerId	InvoiceDate	BillingAddress	Total
1	2	1/1/2018	Billing Address 2	$1.00
2	2	2/1/2018	Billing Address 2	$2.00
3	3	3/1/2018	Billing Address 3	$3.00
4	4	4/1/2018	Billing Address 4	$4.00
5	6	5/1/2017	Billing Address 6	$5.00

INNER JOIN

Simplified Customers Table

CustomerId	Name	Address
1	Customer 1	Address 1
2	Customer 2	Address 2
3	Customer 3	Address 3
4	Customer 4	Address 4
5	Customer 5	Address 6

REMEMBER

As we learned earlier in the chapter, the `CustomerId` field has a one-to-many relationship with the *invoices* table. Although this data may appear mismatched, our result set will return four records. This outcome occurs because Customer 2 created two separate invoices.

The SQL code for this inner join is similar to that of our first example. First, we list the fields we want to display in our SELECT statement, being careful to include the appropriate aliases.

```
SELECT
    i.InvoiceId,
    c.CustomerId,
    c.Name,
    c.Address,
    i.InvoiceDate,
    i.BillingAddress,
    i.Total
FROM
    invoices AS i
INNER JOIN
    customers AS c
ON
    i.CustomerId = c.CustomerId
```

Since inner joins only return matching data, the order that the tables are listed in does not matter. Order *will* matter for other join types.

	InvoiceId	CustomerId	Name	Address	InvoiceDate	BillingAddress	Total
1	1	2	Customer 2	Address 2	1/1/2018	Billing Address 2	$1.00
2	2	2	Customer 2	Address 2	2/1/2018	Billing Address 2	$2.00
3	3	3	Customer 3	Address 3	3/1/2018	Billing Address 3	$3.00
4	4	4	Customer 4	Address 4	4/1/2018	Billing Address 4	$4.00
	4 rows returned in 1ms						

fig. 70

In the output of this query, we can see that only four records were returned. Invoice 5, Customer 1, and Customer 5 are omitted. Customer 2 is responsible for two records.

The inner join is the most common type of join. The main use of an inner join is to bring corresponding data together from different tables in a relational database.

The keyword "inner" is optional on an inner join. All joins are interpreted as inner joins unless otherwise specified. In other words, joins are inner by default.

The Left Outer Join

A left outer join combines all the records from the left table with any matching records from the right table. The Venn diagram equivalent for this type of join is shown in Figure 71.

LEFT OUTER JOIN

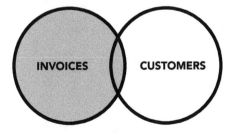

fig. 71

```
SELECT *
FROM invoices AS i
LEFT OUTER JOIN customers AS c
ON i.CustomerId = c.CustomerId
```

The concept of a "left table" and a "right table" depends entirely on the order these tables are listed in a JOIN statement. Switching the listing order will produce a different result set. This distinction will become important when we convert left joins to right joins later in the chapter.

With this type of join, everything in our *invoices* table will be displayed. Since Customer 1 did not order any songs, that particular record is omitted. However, as we can see in Figure 72, we are combining all five records from the *invoices* table with only four records from the *customers* table. (Remember, there is no record for Customers 1 or 5 in the *invoices* table, and Customer 2 produced two invoices.) Unlike the inner join, which matched an equal number of records from each table, a left outer join may return more records from the "left" table. We will have to see the output of this query to understand how the SQL browser handles this.

fig. 72

Simplified Invoices Table

InvoiceId	CustomerId	InvoiceDate	BillingAddress	Total
1	2	1/1/2018	Billing Address 2	$1.00
2	2	2/1/2018	Billing Address 2	$2.00
3	3	3/1/2018	Billing Address 3	$3.00
4	4	4/1/2018	Billing Address 4	$4.00
5	6	5/1/2017	Billing Address 6	$5.00

LEFT JOIN

Simplified Customers Table

CustomerId	Name	Address
1	Customer 1	Address 1
2	Customer 2	Address 2
3	Customer 3	Address 3
4	Customer 4	Address 4
5	Customer 5	Address 6

NULL

The SQL query for a left outer join is very similar to what we used for the inner join. We simply use `LEFT OUTER JOIN` instead.

```
SELECT
    i.InvoiceId,
    c.CustomerId,
    c.Name,
    c.Address,
    i.InvoiceDate,
    i.BillingAddress,
    i.Total
FROM
    invoices AS i
LEFT OUTER JOIN
    customers AS c
ON
    i.CustomerId = c.CustomerId
```

fig. 73

	InvoiceId	CustomerId	Name	Address	InvoiceDate	BillingAddress	Total
1	1	2	Customer 2	Address 2	1/1/2018	Billing Address 2	$1.00
2	2	2	Customer 2	Address 2	2/1/2018	Billing Address 2	$2.00
3	3	3	Customer 3	Address 3	3/1/2018	Billing Address 3	$3.00
4	4	4	Customer 4	Address 4	4/1/2018	Billing Address 4	$4.00
5	5	NULL	NULL	NULL	5/1/2017	Billing Address 6	$5.00
	5 rows returned in 1ms						

With a left outer join, the "outer" keyword is optional.

When we look at the output of our left join, we see that the SQL browser has added null data to our result set. Remember that we have no information in the *customers* table about Customer 6. Adding null data is how the SQL browser handles the fact that we were trying to match five records from *invoices* to only four records from *customers*. Left joins are useful because they allow us to see discrepancies in our data. We can produce lists of customers that have not generated invoices or search for data that has been removed in the right table but still exists in the left table.

The Right Outer Join

Right outer joins are not supported in SQLite, but since right joins are still popular in other RDBMS implementations, we are going to include them anyway. As we mentioned in our discussion of left joins, we will present a workaround for using right joins in SQLite later on.

The right outer join returns the entire right table as well as matching information from the left table. The right join is a mirror image of the left join and functions in a very similar way.

RIGHT OUTER JOIN

fig. 74

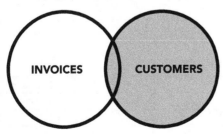

```
SELECT *
FROM invoices AS i
RIGHT OUTER JOIN customers AS c
ON i.CustomerId = c.CustomerId
```

Similar to what occurred with the left join, the right join takes all fields from the right (*customers*) table and matches that data with any corresponding data from the *invoices* table. Since Customer 6 does not exist in the *customers* table, this record is ignored.

fig. 75

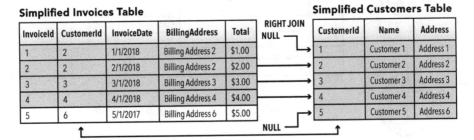

The SQL statement required to create a right join is, not surprisingly, similar to the two other joins we have shown so far.

Just like with the left outer join, the "outer" keyword is optional; simply writing RIGHT JOIN produces the same result.

```
SELECT
    i.InvoiceId,
    c.CustomerId,
    c.Name,
    c.Address,
    i.InvoiceDate,
    i.BillingAddress,
    i.Total
FROM
    invoices AS i
RIGHT OUTER JOIN
    customers AS c
ON
    i.CustomerId = c.CustomerId
```

fig. 76

	InvoiceId	CustomerId	Name	Address	InvoiceDate	BillingAddress	Total
1	NULL	1	Customer 1	Address 1	NULL	NULL	NULL
2	1	2	Customer 2	Address 2	1/1/2018	Billing Address 2	$1.00
3	2	2	Customer 2	Address 2	2/1/2018	Billing Address 2	$2.00
4	3	3	Customer 3	Address 3	3/1/2018	Billing Address 3	$3.00
5	4	4	Customer 4	Address 4	4/1/2017	Billing Address 4	$4.00
6	NULL	5	Customer 5	Address 5	NULL	NULL	NULL
	6 rows returned in 2ms						

This particular join returned the most records out of the three joins we have demonstrated so far. Customers 1 and 5 did not have corresponding data in the *invoices* table, so null values were assigned to those records. Two records from the *invoices* table corresponded to Customer 2, so the join resulted in the data from Customer 2 being listed twice.

Right joins are used less frequently than left joins. Since SQLite does not recognize the right join, it is a best practice is to reverse the order of tables in your query, which yields the same result set. This will be illustrated later in the chapter.

Inner Joins with More Than Two Tables

Joins can combine more than two tables. Adding additional tables using joins is straightforward; it will follow the same pattern as the inner joins we have already demonstrated. Take a look at the database schema in Figure 77. We can see that in addition to the relationship between the *invoices* and *customers* tables, there is also a relationship between the SupportRepId field (from the *customers* table) and the EmployeeId field (from the *employees* table).

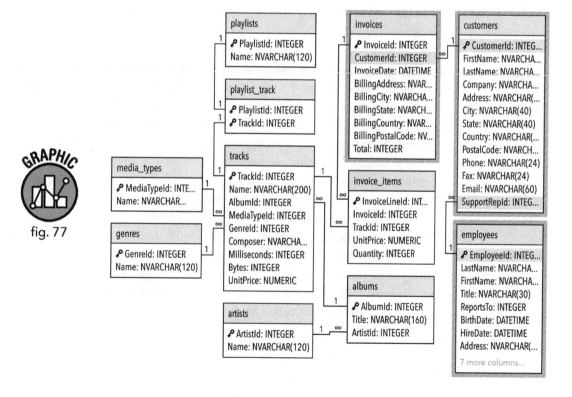

fig. 77

Note that, up to this point, the names of the two fields we have related to each other using the ON keyword have been identical. In this case, we are relating two fields with different names, although the entity relationship diagram shows us that they are corresponding fields. Why does this occur? This disparity teaches us an important lesson about relational database structure. Two corresponding fields don't have to have the same name. There is actually a good reason for these two fields to have different names. In the sTunes company, each customer is assigned a SupportRepId, or a personal company representative. The number assigned to every customer support representative happens to be the same number used for employee number in the *employees* table. The creator of this database could have named both fields EmployeeId, but that strategy could lead to confusion. While it makes sense for customers to have a support representative, and it makes sense that the SupportRepId number is identical to the EmployeeId number, having an EmployeeId field in the *customers* table could cause confusion. The two names, denoting identical data, imply different roles for the data within each table. By naming the field SupportRepId in *customers*, it's immediately clear what this field's purpose is in relation to the *customers* table. Instead of coming up with a different number system for EmployeeId, we can link the two through the power of the relational database structure, and this linkage is notated in the database schema (Figure 77).

Now that we understand how we can relate the *invoices*, *customers*, and *employees* tables, we need to come up with the "why." Let's say the sTunes customer service department wants to reward the employees that are responsible for the ten highest individual sales. Customer service wants to create a plaque for each employee with a list of the customers they have helped. Now that we have an operational scenario, we can look at the ERD to determine what fields we need in our query. Sometimes, when writing complex queries accessing multiple tables, it helps to think through what fields we need and what tables those fields come from (Figure 78).

Now that we have an idea of what fields we want to display, we can begin composing the query. We will start with invoices in our FROM clause. We will then write two INNER JOIN clauses sequentially: one that joins invoices to customers and another that joins both invoices and customers to employees. We will order the entire query by invoice total (in descending order to see the highest totals first).

GRAPHIC
fig. 78

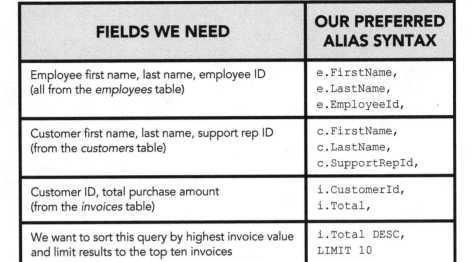

FIELDS WE NEED	OUR PREFERRED ALIAS SYNTAX

Employee first name, last name, employee ID (all from the *employees* table)	`e.FirstName,`
	`e.LastName,`
	`e.EmployeeId,`

Customer first name, last name, support rep ID (from the *customers* table)	`c.FirstName,`
	`c.LastName,`
	`c.SupportRepId,`

Customer ID, total purchase amount (from the *invoices* table)	`i.CustomerId,` `i.Total,`
We want to sort this query by highest invoice value and limit results to the top ten invoices	`i.Total DESC,` `LIMIT 10`

```
SELECT
    e.FirstName,
    e.LastName,
    e.EmployeeId,
    c.FirstName,
    c.LastName,
    c.SupportRepId,
    i.CustomerId,
    i.Total
FROM
    invoices AS i
INNER JOIN
    customers AS c
ON
    i.CustomerId = c.CustomerId
INNER JOIN
    employees AS e
ON
    c.SupportRepId = e.EmployeeId
ORDER BY
    i.Total DESC
LIMIT 10
```

	FirstName	LastName	EmployeeId	FirstName	LastName	SupportRepId	CustomerId	Total
1	Steve	Johnson	5	Helena	Holý	5	6	$25.86
2	Margaret	Park	4	Richard	Cunningham	4	26	$23.86
3	Jane	Peacock	3	Ladislav	Kovács	3	45	$21.86
4	Jane	Peacock	3	Hugh	O'Reilly	3	46	$21.86
5	Steve	Johnson	5	Astrid	Gruber	5	7	$18.86
6	Steve	Johnson	5	Victor	Stevens	5	25	$18.86
7	Steve	Johnson	5	Luís	Rojas	5	57	$17.91
8	Margaret	Park	4	František	Wichterlová	4	5	$16.86
9	Jane	Peacock	3	Isabelle	Mercier	3	43	$16.86
10	Margaret	Park	4	Bjørn	Hansen	4	4	$15.86
	10 rows returned in 5ms							

Now we have a list of sTunes employees responsible for the highest invoice totals. There are a few things we can observe about this result set. As we predicted, even though the fields we use to relate the *customers* table to the *employees* table have two different names, the data clearly corresponds. The number values in `SupportRepId` are the same as the values in the `EmployeeId` field.

ON YOUR OWN:

» Consult the entity relationship diagram and choose another table to add to this query using another inner join. Choose which fields from this new table you wish to display and add them to the select statement.

Using Left Outer Joins with NULL, IS, and NOT

As we saw earlier in the chapter, a left outer join shows us everything from our left table and all matching information from our right table. This ability is useful for analyzing our database and checking for incomplete information. Let's say our sTunes company is conducting an internal audit on the way the company classifies albums versus single songs. sTunes management asks us to generate a list of all artists who do *not* have an album listed. Looking at our preceding entity relationship diagram, we can surmise that the information we are focusing on is going to be stored in the *artists* and *albums* tables. Let's look at the relationship between those tables.

GRAPHIC

fig. 80

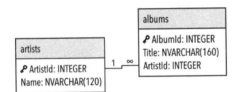

As we can see in Figure 80, our *artists* table consists of an `ArtistId` field, which is our primary key, and a field for the artist name. We can see from the ERD that the *artists* table has a one-to-many relationship with the *albums* table. This relationship makes sense, since an artist can generate many albums. Our *albums* table has its own primary key, `AlbumId`, as well as the `ArtistId` field acting as a foreign key.

A `LEFT OUTER JOIN` with the *artists* table being our left table would return all the data from the *artists* table with matching records (where available) in the *albums* table. Our left join will fill in any fields that do not have album titles with null values. Now that we have a clear plan, we can begin to compose our query.

We have used the first letter of a table as its alias for most joins in this chapter. Since we have two tables with the same first letter, we will use two letters for each in this query.

```
SELECT
    ar.ArtistId AS [ArtistId From Artists Table],
    al.ArtistId AS [ArtistId From Albums Table],
    ar.Name AS [Artist Name],
    al.Title AS [Album Title]
FROM
    artists AS ar
LEFT OUTER JOIN
    albums AS al
ON
    ar.ArtistId = al.ArtistId
```

At first, when we scan through the 418 records returned by this query, nothing seems out of place. The `ArtistId` field from the *artists* table seems to match the `ArtistId` field from the *albums* table. Most artist names are associated with album titles. However, if we scroll down farther in our result set (Figure 81), we begin to see null values appear.

To fully answer our initial inquiry and retrieve all artists who do not have an album, we would need to add a `WHERE` clause that specified only the records that are null in the *albums* table. There are specific SQL keywords we use to work with null values.

» `IS NULL` in a `WHERE` clause would return only values that were null
» `NOT NULL` would return only values that were not null

	ArtistId From Artists Table	ArtistId From Albums Table	Artist Name	Album	
...	...	...	...	...	...
51	25	NULL	Milton Nascimento & Bebeto	NULL	
52	26	NULL	Azymuth	NULL	
53	27	27	Gilberto Gil	As Canções de Eu Tu Eles	
54	27	27	Gilberto Gil	Quanta Gente Veio Ver (Live)	
55	27	27	Gilberto Gil	Quanta Gente Veio ver–Bônus De Carnaval	
56	28	NULL	João Gilberto	NULL	
57	29	NULL	Bebel Gilberto	NULL	
58	30	NULL	Jorge Vercilo	NULL	
59	31	NULL	Baby Consuelo	NULL	
60	32	NULL	Ney Matogrosso	NULL	
...	418 rows returned in 18ms				

fig. 81

Adding a clause that specifies that we are only looking for cases `WHERE al.ArtistId IS NULL` would return a list of artists without album names.

We must use `IS` and `NOT` when dealing with nulls rather than the equals sign "=" operator. Nulls represent a lack of data. The = operator compares the value of two items. Nulls have no value and thus cannot be compared using the = operator. Attempting to use = will produce an error.

```
SELECT
    ar.ArtistId AS [ArtistId From Artists Table],
    al.ArtistId AS [ArtistId From Albums Table],
    ar.Name AS [Artist Name],
    al.Title AS [Album]
FROM
    artists AS ar
LEFT OUTER JOIN
    albums AS al
ON
    ar.ArtistId = al.ArtistId
WHERE
    al.ArtistId IS NULL
```

In our result set (Figure 82), we have 71 records where there are no corresponding albums next to the artist name.

fig. 82

	ArtistId From Artists Table	ArtistId From Albums Table	Artist Name	Album
1	25	NULL	Milton Nascimento & Bebeto	NULL
2	26	NULL	Azymuth	NULL
3	28	NULL	João Gilberto	NULL
4	29	NULL	Bebel Gilberto	NULL
5	30	NULL	Jorge Vercilo	NULL
6	31	NULL	Baby Consuelo	NULL
7	32	NULL	Ney Matogrosso	NULL
8	33	NULL	Luiz Melodia	NULL
9	34	NULL	Nando Reis	NULL
10	35	NULL	Pedro Luís & A Parede	NULL
...	71 rows returned in 1ms			

Turning a Right Join into a Left Join

As we learned earlier in the chapter, right joins are not supported in SQLite. We also learned that right joins are mirror images of left joins. Consider the Venn diagram below.

A right join takes all records on the right side and joins them with all corresponding records from the left. If you simply switch the left and right tables, then you can use a left outer join to the very same effect. The following query has been written as a right outer join. This query takes any corresponding album or title info from the *albums* table and merges it with *all* records from the *tracks* table.

```
SELECT * FROM albums AS al RIGHT OUTER JOIN tracks
AS t ON t.AlbumId = al.AlbumId
```

is the same as

```
SELECT * FROM tracks AS t LEFT OUTER JOIN albums
AS al ON t.AlbumId = al.AlbumId
```

fig. 83

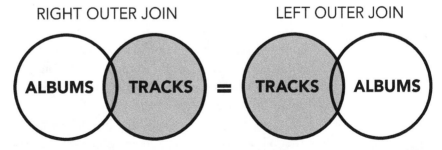

ALBUMS RIGHT JOIN TRACKS = TRACKS LEFT JOIN ALBUMS

```
SELECT
    t.TrackId,
    t.Composer,
    t.Name,
    al.AlbumId,
    al.Title
FROM
    albums AS al
RIGHT OUTER JOIN
    tracks AS t
ON
    t.AlbumId = al.AlbumId
```

If you run the preceding query in DB Browser, you will get the following error: RIGHT and FULL OUTER JOINs are not currently supported.

That isn't a problem for us, however, as we know that by simply swapping the two table names in the join, we can achieve the same result. Consider the following query; the only thing that differs from the query above is the order in which the tables are listed:

```
SELECT
    t.TrackId,
    t.Composer,
    t.Name,
    al.AlbumId,
    al.Title
FROM
    tracks AS t
LEFT OUTER JOIN
    albums AS al
ON
    t.AlbumId = al.AlbumId
```

Now this query can be run, and we can observe the results (Figure 84). With this query we can see the composer of a song, the song name, and the album title all in one result set. We can also observe that there are some null values in the composer field. From there, we could rewrite the query to investigate those null values. The key takeaway from left/right joins is that they allow you to "troubleshoot" your own databases and really discover inconsistencies in your data. If you are looking for corresponding data and are willing to risk omitting a few records due to database errors, it is better to just use an inner join.

	TrackId	Composer	Name	AlbumId	Title
1	1	Angus Young, Malcolm Young, Brian Johnson	For Those About To Rock (We Salute You)	1	For Those About To Rock (We Salute You)
2	2	NULL	Balls to the Wall	2	Balls to the Wall
3	3	F. Baltes, S. Kaufman, U. Dirkscneider & W. Hoffman	Fast As a Shark	3	Restless and Wild
4	4	F. Baltes, R.A. Smith-Diesel, S. Kaufman, U. Dirkscneider & W. Hoffman	Restless and Wild	3	Restless and Wild
5	5	Deaffy & R.A. Smith-Diesel	Princess of the Dawn	3	Restless and Wild
6	6	Angus Young, Malcolm Young, Brian Johnson	Put The Finger On You	1	For Those About To Rock (We Salute You)
7	7	Angus Young, Malcolm Young, Brian Johnson	Let's Get It Up	1	For Those About To Rock (We Salute You)
8	8	Angus Young, Malcolm Young, Brian Johnson	Inject The Venom	1	For Those About To Rock (We Salute You)
9	9	Angus Young, Malcolm Young, Brian Johnson	Snowballed	1	For Those About To Rock (We Salute You)
10	10	Angus Young, Malcolm Young, Brian Johnson	Evil Walks	1	For Those About To Rock (We Salute You)
...	3503 rows returned in 25ms				

fig. 84

ON YOUR OWN:

» Modify the above query to display only the records where the `Composer` field is null.

Data Analysis Checkpoint

1. Using DB Browser and the Browse Data tab or the entity relationship diagram in Figure 65, view the *tracks* table. Identify which fields in that table are foreign keys in another table. Based on the foreign keys you have identified, which tables are related to the *tracks* table?

2. Create an inner join between the *albums* and *tracks* tables and display the album names and track names in a single result set.

3. Using the *genres* table identified from question 1, create a third inner join to join to this table and include the `Name` field from that table in your result set.

Chapter Recap

» Joins harness the power of a relational database to bring data together from different tables.

» Use of an entity relationship diagram is helpful when writing joins.

» When selecting fields from multiple tables at once, aliases are needed to specify the table of origin.

» Inner joins do not include rows where there is no corresponding data.

» Outer joins include all rows of one of the tables, even when there is no corresponding data between tables. Rows that do not match will show up as null.

» The special keywords IS and NOT must be used to test for null values.

» Right joins can be used in implementations of SQL other than SQLite. To do the equivalent of a right join in SQLite, simply switch the position of the two tables you are comparing in your query statement.

| 7 |
Using Functions

Chapter Overview
» Adding calculations to your queries
» Types of functions in SQL
» String functions
» Date functions
» Aggregate functions
» Using the WHERE and HAVING clauses with functions
» Grouping by multiple columns
» Data Analysis Checkpoint

If you have been testing your knowledge using our end-of-chapter Data Analysis Checkpoints, you may have noticed that a few of the questions required an additional step to be performed after you wrote your query. For example, at the end of chapter 4, we asked you "How many of our customer's last names start with *B*?" Other questions asked you to find totals of invoices within a certain price range. Using the tools you had available at the time, some of these questions required you to manually count or add up the query results in order to obtain the answer. To calculate all last names ending in *B* using only knowledge from chapter 4, you could select the LastName field from the *customers* table, order by last name, scroll down to the *B* names, then count those names manually. If you augmented your query with chapter 5 knowledge, you could make the task a bit easier by restricting the dataset to return only last names starting with *B* (using WHERE LastName LIKE 'B%'). However, you would still have to do the count manually. This chapter will show you how to simplify your calculations by using functions.

Adding Calculations to Your Queries
Calculations (like counting the number of records returned), can be performed by adding functions to our queries. With the use of a function called COUNT(), we can ask the SQL browser to do a count of LastName

and use an alias to return the value as NameCount. Adding a function to a basic SELECT statement would look something like this:

```
SELECT
    COUNT(LastName) AS [NameCount]
FROM
    customers
WHERE
    LastName LIKE 'B%'
```

fig. 85

	NameCount
1	4
	1 rows returned in 2ms

Instead of listing all the entries starting with *B*, (which we would then have to count), we could use the COUNT() function to add up all fields in the *customers* table that satisfy our WHERE condition. The end result gives us an aliased field and the number of last names starting with *B*.

This is just one example of how functions can save us time by doing some of the extra work for us. In this chapter, we will go over three different types of functions in SQL and give examples of the ones that are the most useful.

Types of Functions in SQL

Functions in SQL are special keywords that accept certain parameters, perform an operation (such as a calculation or modification of the data in the field), and return the result of that operation as a value. You have already had a sneak preview of functions in chapter 5, where we introduced the DATE() function. The DATE() function took as its parameter data in the format DATETIME, performed an operation (stripped the time stamp portion away), and then returned only the date portion of the data point. But as we mentioned in chapter 5, there are many more types of functions in SQL that do a variety of tasks. Figure 86 contains a list of some of the most common and useful ones.

This list is by no means exhaustive. All of the functions mentioned in this book are ones specifically recognized by SQLite. Other database implementations have different functions. A full list of functions understood by SQLite is available on the SQLite webpage.[10]

TYPES OF FUNCTIONS

STRING	DATE	AGGREGATE
INSTR()	DATE()	AVG()
LENGTH()	DATETIME()	COUNT()
LOWER()	JULIANDAY()	MAX()
LTRIM()	STRFTIME()	MIN()
REPLACE()	TIME()	SUM()
RTRIM()	'NOW'	
SUBSTR()		
TRIM()	←——— || (double pipes concatenation)
UPPER()		

fig. 86

As you can see in Figure 86, the functions we cover in this book come in three different types:

> » **String functions** modify character and text-based data.
> » **Date functions** modify time and date data.
> » **Aggregate functions** perform mathematical operations.

Functions in SQL operate very similar to the way functions operate in spreadsheet software and other programming languages. If you have ever used the SUM() feature in a Microsoft Excel spreadsheet, then you will already have some idea of how to use functions. Another similarity these functions share with Excel functions is the "pop-up" style definitions that appear once we type the function in the SQL browser. Consider this example. In the Execute SQL Pane, start to type the name of a function with one open bracket:

```
UPPER(
```

After doing this, you should see the following text pop up under the function you just typed:

```
The UPPER(X) function returns a copy of input
string X in which all lowercase ASCII characters
are converted to their uppercase equivalent.
```

The portion of the function in parentheses (X) is called the argument of the function. Some functions may take more than one argument.

Most functions in DB Browser have pop-up information that is very helpful for determining what ***argument(s)*** the function takes and what the function actually does. Try a few others for yourself.

ON YOUR OWN:

» The UPPER() function takes only one argument (X). How many arguments does the REPLACE() function take?

» According to the tooltip (onscreen in DB Browser), what does the TRIM() function do?

If you do not see the pop-up, make sure you are typing the function correctly. The function pop-up text will not appear if you just copy and paste the function and the open parenthesis into the Execute Pane. This is another reason you should always type queries by hand. No shortcuts!

Manipulating Text Data with String Functions

A *string* is another word for text data stored in a text-based data type. String functions can format and modify text. To understand how string functions operate, we need to conduct a brief refresher on data types in SQLite. In chapter 3, while investigating the structure of our database, we observed that the text-based data was saved in a format called NVARCHAR(X). NVARCHAR is a variable-length string where the X represents the maximum length of the string.

For character data with a fixed length (like postal codes with letters in them), a different fixed-length data type can be used. However, in the sTunes database, the character data type NVARCHAR is used for all text-based data.

Being able to manipulate text strings is important because the fields in a database are not always organized in a way that is most useful to us. Let's say we were asked to create a mailing list of our US customers. To do this we would need their names and addresses. We can get that easily with a quick SELECT statement.

```
SELECT
    FirstName,
    LastName,
    Address
FROM
    customers
WHERE
    Country = 'USA'
```

Running this query returns the following—but there is a slight problem.

fig. 87

	FirstName	LastName	Address
1	Frank	Harris	1600 Amphitheatre Parkway
2	Jack	Smith	1 Microsoft Way
3	Michelle	Brooks	627 Broadway
4	Tim	Goyer	1 Infinite Loop
5	Dan	Miller	541 Del Medio Avenue
...	13 rows returned in 5ms		

The address data is split up into parts. Simply requesting the Address field is not enough. We would also need to select the City, State, and PostalCode fields. The other issue is that all this data is in separate fields. If you want to create a simple mailing list, where each line represents the customer's full name and address, then the current layout is formatted very poorly for that.

ON YOUR OWN:
» Try copying the output from the last query into DB Browser in a text editor. What does it look like?

Fortunately, there are some great tools for manipulating text strings so that we can get the output looking the way we want it. The first of these tools is called concatenation.

Concatenating Strings of Text

Joining fields together is called concatenating them. To add two fields together we use a two-pipe || operator. For example, if we wanted to concatenate the fields FirstName and LastName, we could write the following:

```
SELECT
    FirstName || LastName
FROM
    customers
WHERE
    CustomerId = 1
```

This would give us the following output:

fig. 88

	FirstName || LastName
1	LuísGonçalves
	1 rows returned in 1ms

You can see from the output of our concatenation query that the || operator merely attached both fields together without spaces. To make this output a bit cleaner, we can use two concatenations in sequence and include a space in single quotation marks. After making this adjustment, our query looks like the following:

```
SELECT
    FirstName,
    LastName,
    FirstName || ' ' || LastName
FROM
    customers
WHERE
    Country = "USA"
```

We should get output that looks like this:

	FirstName	LastName	FirstName || LastName
1	Frank	Harris	Frank Harris
2	Jack	Smith	Jack Smith
3	Michelle	Brooks	Michelle Brooks
4	Tim	Goyer	Tim Goyer
5	Dan	Miller	Dan Miller
...	13 rows returned in 1ms		

fig. 89

ON YOUR OWN:
» When you run this query for yourself, make things a little cleaner by creating an alias called "Full Name" for our concatenated field.

The concatenation function || doesn't really look like the rest of the functions we will be exploring in this chapter. In other implementations of SQL, there is an actual CONCAT() function. Still other implementations use a + symbol. The syntax may be different depending on which RDBMS you use, but the effect is the same.

Now that we have seen an example, we can use multiple concatenations to create a one-line name and address list for all our customers.

```
SELECT
    FirstName || ' ' || LastName || ' ' || Address
    || ', ' || City || ', ' || State || ' ' ||
    PostalCode AS [MailingAddress]
FROM
    customers
WHERE
    Country = "USA"
```

The result looks like this:

GRAPHIC

fig. 90

	MailingAddress
1	Frank Harris 1600 Amphitheatre Parkway, Mountain View, CA 94043-1351
2	Jack Smith 1 Microsoft Way, Redmond, WA 98052-8300
3	Michelle Brooks 627 Broadway, New York, NY 10012-2612
4	Tim Goyer 1 Infinite Loop, Cupertino, CA 95014
5	Dan Miller 541 Del Medio Avenue, Mountain View, CA 94040-111
...	13 rows returned in 5ms

ON YOUR OWN:

» When you run this query, try pasting the output from DB Browser into a text editor to see how different it looks. The output should look much cleaner than before we concatenated it.

NOTE

You do not have to use only spaces in between the double pipes. In the previous example, we used a comma and then a space ', ' to get the desired format. You can add any text you wish as long as you put it inside the quotation marks.

Truncating Text

We can also separate or truncate text using functions. Looking at the example above, you can see that the US postal codes in our *customers* table are not uniform. Some of them include a hyphen and an additional four-digit number, referred to by the US Postal Service as a ZIP+4 code. And one of the postal codes seems to be missing the fourth digit of the ZIP+4 code.

MY TAKE

This is a good time to mention that finding errors or inconsistencies in a database is inevitable. Being able to anticipate and handle errors and exceptions is part of the learning process and an invaluable skill. Fields often have misspellings, an incorrect number of characters, or other issues. Over time you will learn to anticipate and handle errors as you come across them.

We can use functions to remove the hyphen and extra numbers so that our postal code output is uniform. Thanks to the US Postal Service's advanced routing system, the additional numbers in US postal codes (beyond the initial five) are not required.

To use string editing functions, we need to know a bit more about how strings are saved in a database. The characters in every string are numbered starting with 1. This becomes important when we start manipulating strings because it allows us to specify what parts we want to manipulate based on the character number.

If we use the LENGTH() function on a field like PostalCode from our *customers* table, we can see that the length of each code is calculated.

```
SELECT
    PostalCode,
    LENGTH(PostalCode) AS [Postal Code Length]
FROM
    customers
WHERE
    Country = "USA"
```

fig. 91

PostalCode	Postal Code Length
94043-1351	10
98052-8300	10
10012-2612	10
95014	5
94040-111	9
89503	5
32801	5
2113	4
60611	5
53703	5
...	13 rows returned in 1ms

Looking at the output (Figure 91), it is easy to see that our postal codes vary in string size. The minimum necessary length of a US postal code is five digits. Let's remove all information after the fifth position in the string. We can do this with the SUBSTR() function.

The SUBSTR() function exists in two forms: SUBSTR(X,Y) and SUBSTR(X,Y,Z). As we have done before, we can type "SUBSTR(" into our browser for a brief description of how it works.

To get DB Browser to give you a pop-up preview of SUBSTR(X,Y,Z), you will need to type "SUBSTR(X,Y," to tell the browser you are interested in the three-argument version of this function.

GRAPHIC

fig. 92

FUNCTION	DESCRIPTION
SUBSTR(X,Y)	Returns all characters through the end of the string X beginning with the Y-th.
SUBSTR(X,Y,Z)	Returns a substring of input string X that begins with the Y-th character and that is Z characters long.

If we use the SUBSTR(X,Y,Z) function to remove the extra data from the US postal codes, the X will be our PostalCode field, and the Y argument specifies the starting position of the string. In this case, we want the first five numbers to remain, so we are going to choose 1. The Z argument specifies the number of characters the function will return from the starting position, which in our case is five.

If we select only the United States addresses and then include the SUBSTR(X,Y,Z) function with an alias, we get the following:

```
SELECT
    PostalCode,
    SUBSTR(PostalCode,1,5) AS [Five Digit Postal
    Code]
FROM
    customers
WHERE
    Country = "USA"
```

Looking at the output (Figure 93), we can see that all our postal codes retain only the first five digits.

NOTE

The postal codes that never had the additional numbers aren't affected by this query.

Using the SUBSTR() function, we can also split data apart. Note that the version of SUBSTR() that takes two arguments returns all characters through the end of the string beginning with the Y-th. If our Y value doesn't start at character 1, we can direct the function to only return characters from the Y-th character and onward.

fig. 93

PostalCode	Five Digit Postal Code
94043-1351	94043
98052-8300	98052
10012-2612	10012
95014	95014
94040-111	94040
89503	89503
32801	32801
2113	2113
60611	60611
53703	53703
...	13 rows returned in 1ms

ON YOUR OWN:

» Repeat the preceding SQL statement but add an additional field to the SELECT portion of the query using SUBSTR(X,Y) that includes only the last four digits of the postal code (where available) with the alias "ZIP+4 Code."

Additional String Functions

The functions listed in this text are by no means exhaustive. As mentioned in the beginning of this chapter, a full list of SQLite supported functions can be found on the SQLite website. An alternative way to learn new functions is to type them in, read the tooltip, and try to figure out how they work. Before we move on to date and aggregate functions, we will introduce two more string functions that are very useful.

fig. 94

FUNCTION	DESCRIPTION
UPPER()	Returns a copy of input string X in which all lowercase ASCII characters are converted to their uppercase equivalent.
LOWER()	Returns a copy of string X with all ASCII characters converted to lowercase.

As we saw earlier looking at the tooltip, the UPPER(X) function returns a copy of input string X in which all lowercase ASCII characters are converted to their uppercase equivalent. The LOWER() function enacts a similar process. The following SQL statement demonstrates both of these functions.

```
SELECT
    FirstName as [First Name Unmodified],
    UPPER(FirstName) as [First Name in UPPERCASE],
    LOWER(FirstName) as [First Name in lowercase],
    UPPER(FirstName) || ' ' || UPPER(LastName) AS
    [Full Name in UPPERCASE]
FROM
    customers
```

In this query, we passed the entire FirstName field into the UPPER() and LOWER() functions as an argument, and then used an alias to label the result. We also created a "Full Name" alias to show that you can concatenate two fields after performing functions on them.

GRAPHIC

fig. 95

	First Name Unmodified	First Name in UPPERCASE	First Name in lowercase	Full Name in UPPERCASE
1	Luís	LUÍS	luís	LUÍS GONÇALVES
2	Leonie	LEONIE	leonie	LEONIE KöHLER
3	François	FRANçOIS	françois	FRANçOIS TREMBLAY
4	Bjørn	BJøRN	bjørn	BJøRN HANSEN
5	František	FRANTIšEK	františek	FRANTIšEK WICHTERLOVá
6	Helena	HELENA	helena	HELENA HOLý
7	Astrid	ASTRID	astrid	ASTRID GRUBER
8	Daan	DAAN	daan	DAAN PEETERS
9	Kara	KARA	kara	KARA NIELSEN
10	Eduardo	EDUARDO	eduardo	EDUARDO MARTINS
...	59 rows returned in 3ms			

NOTE

The upper and lower functions only work on ASCII characters. Any characters initially formatted in unicode are left unchanged.

ON YOUR OWN:

» Use the SUBSTR() function together with the case functions and create a list of customers with the last name listed first in capital letters and only the first initial of the first name.

Date Functions

Date functions allow us to manipulate data stored in various date and time formats. In our sTunes database, the date information is stored in a `DATETIME` format: `YYYY-MM-DD HH:MM:SS`. Although the format gives us space for a timecode, the timecode is not being used in our database and all of the timecodes are blank and show 00:00:00. Because of this, we have used the `DATE()` function (first introduced in chapter 5), to strip away the timecode and leave us with just the date information. Since date information can be stored in different ways in any given database, it is important to know how to convert one format to another. There is a lot more we can do with dates other than just changing their formats. For example, we can get the difference between any given date and the current date to calculate the ages of our employees, since we have a `BirthDate` field in the *employees* table.

In order to calculate employee ages, we will need to learn a bit more about the `STRFTIME()` function, also known as the string format time function. As the name implies, this function formats the time and date information as a text string. The `STRFTIME()` function needs at least two pieces of information to operate correctly. You must provide your desired format (also known as a conversion specification) and a timestring to format. The timestring can be a `DATETIME` field from your database or it can be typed manually. The timestring can also use the `NOW` function as an argument. The third argument, a modifier, is optional and can be used to incrementally shift the date forward or back and perform a few other functions.

FUNCTION	DESCRIPTION
STRFTIME()	STRFTIME(format, timestring, modifier, modifier, ...) Converts date and time to a string. STRFTIME() takes a format (or "conversion specifications"), a timestring, and as many (optional) modifiers as desired.
'NOW'	This function takes no argument. Using the NOW function returns the current time when it is executed. STRFTIME(), DATE(), and other time functions can take NOW as an argument.

GRAPHIC

fig. 96

NOTE

The NOW function is sometimes called a nondeterministic function, which is a fancy way of saying that the resulting data returned from this function is different every time it is called, since the date and/or time will be different every time it is called. The STRFTIME() function and most other functions covered in this book are deterministic; that is, they produce the same result every time they are used with the same arguments. The NOW function needs to be constantly updated so it relies on your computer's time to stay accurate.

ARGUMENTS FOR STRFTIME

In specific order: format, timestring, modifier (optional)

GRAPHIC

fig. 97

(format) These are case-sensitive	DESCRIPTION
'%d'	day of month: 00
'%f'	fractional seconds: SS.SSS
'%H'	hour: 00-24
'%j'	day of year: 001-366
'%J'	Julian day number
'%m'	month: 01-12
'%M'	minute: 00-59
'%s'	seconds since 1970-01-01
'%S'	seconds: 00-59
'%w'	day of week 0-6 with Sunday=0
'%W'	week of year: 00-53
'%Y'	year: 0000-9999

GRAPHIC

fig. 98

(timestring)	DESCRIPTION
'YYYY-MM-DD'	A date typed in Year-Month-Day format.
'now'	The current date and time.
'DATETIME' field	A database field in a date and/or time format.

fig. 99

(modifier)	DESCRIPTION
'+ X days'	Where X is the number of days to add to the result.
'+ X months'	Where X is the number of months to add to the result.
'+ X years'	Where X is the number of years to add to the result.
'- X days'/months/years	Where X is the number of days/months/years to subtract from the result.
'start of day'	Modifies the time code to represent the beginning of the day.
'start of month'	Modifies the month value to the first of the month.
'start of year'	Modifies the datecode to represent the first day of the year.

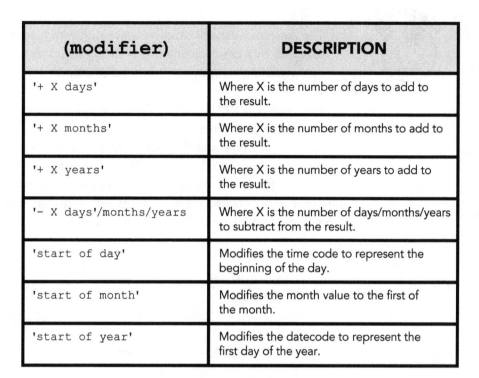

We can see from Figures 97, 98, and 99 that the STRFTIME() function lends itself to extensive modification. If you do not understand the significance of all the arguments and modifications STRFTIME() can take, don't worry. At its core, STRFTIME() takes time and date formatted data and uses keywords to return the user-specified portions of the date.

As we have seen in other text strings, we can use any characters we like inside the single quotation marks, provided we include quotation marks around the entire string.

```
SELECT
STRFTIME('The Year is: %Y The Day is: %d The Month
is %m', '2011-05-22') AS [Text with Conversion
Specifications]
```

fig. 100

	Text with Conversion Specifications
1	The Year is: 2011 The Day is: 22 The Month is 05
	1 rows returned in 1ms

The conversion specifications always start with the % symbol followed by a case-sensitive letter. Using an uppercase %M instead of %m would give us minutes instead of months.

Let's use STRFTIME() to calculate employee ages. The first thing to do is to specify the format we desire returned to us. Since BirthDate is a DATETIME data type and the timecodes are blank in our database, we have no interest in the timecodes so we will omit them for the sake of clarity. Since we want to figure out the age of our employees, we want to calculate the difference in time between a given employee's birthdate and the present date. The present date is provided by the NOW function.

```
SELECT
    LastName,
    FirstName,
    STRFTIME('%Y-%m-%d',BirthDate) AS [Birthday No
    Timecode],
    STRFTIME('%Y-%m-%d','now') - STRFTIME('%Y-%m-%d',
    BirthDate) AS [Age]
FROM
    employees
ORDER BY
    Age
```

fig. 101

	LastName	FirstName	Birthday No Timecode	Age
1	Peacock	Jane	8/29/1973	46
2	Mitchell	Michael	7/1/1973	46
3	King	Robert	5/29/1970	49
4	Callahan	Laura	1/9/1968	51
5	Johnson	Steve	3/3/1965	54
6	Adams	Andrew	2/18/1962	57
7	Edwards	Nancy	12/8/1958	61
8	Park	Margaret	9/19/1947	72
	8 rows returned in 1ms			

As you can see from the results, we can use STRFTIME() in the same way we used the DATE() function to strip off timecodes. We then get the difference between two strftime functions in order to get employee age.

ON YOUR OWN:

» sTunes celebrates employee birthdays on the first of the month. Create a table for HR that shows employee names, birthdays, and the celebration day.

» sTunes Human Resources has told us that employee age is a sensitive topic. Rewrite this exercise by listing employees by number of years with the company.

» Which employee has been with the company the longest?

Aggregate Functions

Aggregate functions can turn a range of numbers into a single data point based on a variety of mathematical operations. At the beginning of this chapter, we used the COUNT() function to find the total number of all customers with last name starting with *B*. There are many more helpful ways to use aggregate functions. As an example, using our invoices table, we can use the SUM() function to calculate a total of all invoices.

```
SELECT
    SUM(Total) AS [Total Sales]
FROM
    invoices
```

Although there are many aggregate functions,[11] let's focus on five basic ones that we should be aware of in SQL: SUM(), AVG(), MIN(), MAX(), and COUNT().

GRAPHIC

fig. 102

FUNCTION	DESCRIPTION
SUM()	Returns the sum of all non-null values.
AVG()	Returns the average value of all non-null values.
MIN()	Returns the minimum value of all non-null values.
MAX()	Returns the maximum value of all non-null values.
COUNT()	Returns a count of all non-null values.

If we run the following statement:

```
SELECT
    SUM(Total) AS TotalSales,
    AVG(Total) AS AverageSales,
    MAX(Total) AS MaximumSale,
    MIN(Total) AS MinSale,
    COUNT(*) AS SalesCount
FROM
    invoices
```

We get the following output:

GRAPHIC

	TotalSales	AverageSales	MaximumSale	MinSale	SalesCount
1	"2328.6"	"5.651941..."	"25.86"	"0.99"	"412"
	1 rows returned in 2ms				

fig. 103

NOTE

By default, the COUNT() function returns only values that are not null. However, if we want a count of all records, even records with errors or nulls, it is a best practice to use the asterisk * or primary key field. The asterisk symbolizes "return all records," so when it is used with the COUNT() aggregate function, we are asking for a count of all records in the *invoices* table.

ON YOUR OWN:

» How many invoices are in our *invoices* table?
» What is the average invoice amount?
» What is the amount of the largest invoice in our table?

Nesting Functions with the ROUND() Function

A nested function is a function contained within another function. One reason we would want to nest functions is to further modify the format of the inner function. If we look at the example above where we used the AVG() function, we see that "Average Sales" contains too many decimal places to be used as a monetary value. The ROUND() function, although not considered an aggregate function, is very useful when we perform any sort of mathematical operation and we want to tidy up our results. We can accomplish this by placing the AVG() function inside the ROUND() function (also known as nesting), and specifying the number of decimals we want the function to round to.

fig. 104

FUNCTION	DESCRIPTION
ROUND(X,Y)	Returns a floating point value X rounded to Y digits to the right of the decimal point. If the Y argument is omitted, it is assumed to be 0.

```
SELECT
    AVG(Total) AS [Average Sales],
    ROUND(AVG(Total), 2) AS [Rounded Average Sales]
FROM
    invoices
```

fig. 105

	Average Sales	Rounded Average Sales
1	5.65194174757283	5.65
	1 rows returned in 1ms	

When using the ROUND() function with monetary values, you may want to be careful of rounding up prematurely and changing monetary values during intermediary calculations. Usually, rounding is only done at the last step, and you can annotate your query with comments to state that the results are rounded to two decimal places.

Using Aggregate Functions with the GROUP BY Clause

A useful feature of aggregate functions is their ability to calculate subtotals or aggregates for different groups of data. Looking at the *invoices* table of our sTunes database, we know that we can get the average amount of an invoice very easily with the AVG() function. Let's say that our sTunes company asks us to calculate the average invoice amount by billing city. To attempt to answer that question, we construct the following query.

CAUTION

The following query has been written incorrectly to show what happens when you combine aggregate functions with non-aggregate fields in your SELECT statement. This query produces no errors, but it does not correctly display the information we are requesting.

```
SELECT
    BillingCity,
    AVG(Total)
FROM
    invoices
ORDER BY
    BillingCity
```

If you run this query, you will see that something is wrong.

GRAPHIC

	BillingCity	AVG(Total)
1	Delhi	5.65194174757283
	1 rows returned in 1ms	

fig. 106

We wanted to view the average invoice amount of each individual city's *invoices* table. Even though we included billing city in our SELECT statement, the query is still only giving us a global average of all invoices. Why isn't our query returning the average total for every city in our *invoices* table?

To solve this puzzle, let's look at what we are asking the SQL browser to do. The question we were asked was "What are the average invoice totals by city?"

REMEMBER

When we first introduced queries in chapter 4, we explained that it is often helpful to break a query down into its components and ask "What table contains the information I need?" and "How do I want that information displayed?" Asking these two questions can help you troubleshoot a query that is not returning the information you expected.

In the preceding incorrect query, we asked the SQL browser for two items in the *invoices* table. First, we asked the browser to list every city in the BillingCity field. Then, we asked the browser to give us an average of the Total field. The former request yields a multi-line response, and the latter gives a one-line answer. In other words, we are asking the browser to display both aggregate and non-aggregate fields at the same time. We did not get the information we wanted because we did not phrase our question correctly.

We can fix this issue by adding the GROUP BY clause to the query, as follows:

```
SELECT
    BillingCity,
    AVG(Total)
FROM
    invoices
GROUP BY
    BillingCity
ORDER BY
    BillingCity
```

fig. 107

	BillingCity	AVG(Total)
1	Amsterdam	5.802857143
2	Bangalore	6.106666667
3	Berlin	5.374285714
4	Bordeaux	5.66
5	Boston	5.374285714
...	53 rows returned in 2ms	

When we execute the query (Figure 107), we observe that all billing cities now occur once in our result set and display the corresponding *average* subtotals for each city.

ON YOUR OWN:
» When you run this query, add the ROUND() function to clean up the averages to two decimal points.

Using the WHERE and HAVING Clauses with Grouped Queries

Adding criteria to a grouped query works in the same way as with other queries we have seen. Using the WHERE clause allows us to add new criteria. In our example below, criteria are added for the non-aggregated field BillingCity.

```
SELECT
    BillingCity,
    AVG(Total)
FROM
    invoices
WHERE
    BillingCity LIKE 'L%'
GROUP BY
    BillingCity
ORDER BY
    BillingCity
```

GRAPHIC

fig. 108

	BillingCity	AVG(Total)
1	Lisbon	5.66
2	London	5.374285714
3	Lyon	5.374285714
	3 rows returned in 1ms	

REMEMBER

A non-aggregate field is just a field in the SELECT clause that is called out without an aggregate function.

ON YOUR OWN:

» In the previous query, how many billing cities begin with *L*?

In the last example, we added criteria to a non-aggregate field. At times we will want to use criteria on fields that have been aggregated, like AVG(Total). For instance, what if we were asked to find all average totals that are less than 20. We could attempt to answer this with a WHERE clause, but there is a problem.

CAUTION

The following SQL statement contains an error. But it is important to see that criteria created by the WHERE clause do not work with aggregate data.

```
SELECT
    BillingCity,
    AVG(Total)
FROM
    invoices
```

```
WHERE
    AVG(Total) > 5
GROUP BY
    BillingCity
ORDER BY
    BillingCity
```

If you run this query, you will get the following error message:

```
Misuse of aggregate: AVG():
```

This error message tells us that—at least in this case—we cannot use the WHERE clause to create a condition based on an aggregate function. In this case, the WHERE clause can only direct the query about what information to pull from the fields in our SELECT clause. If we want additional filtering based on aggregate functions, we will have to include a secondary filtering clause, known as the HAVING clause.

The HAVING clause always comes after the GROUP BY clause. Our query is modified to look as follows:

```
SELECT
    BillingCity,
    AVG(Total)
FROM
    invoices
GROUP BY
    BillingCity
HAVING
    AVG(Total) > 5
ORDER BY
    BillingCity
```

fig. 109

	BillingCity	AVG(Total)
1	Amsterdam	5.802857143
2	Bangalore	6.106666667
3	Berlin	5.374285714
4	Bordeaux	5.66
5	Boston	5.374285714
...	53 rows returned in 2ms	

The WHERE Clause Versus the HAVING Clause

A very simplified explanation of the difference between the WHERE clause and the HAVING clause is that WHERE is for filtering non-aggregate data and HAVING is for filtering results containing aggregates. A more detailed way to describe this difference is that two types of filtering occur when both a WHERE clause and a HAVING clause are included in a query. The WHERE clause tells the query what information to include from the table, then, once the information is filtered and aggregate functions are applied to the fields, the HAVING clause acts as a further filter for the aggregated data. To demonstrate this, let's repeat the query above, but this time let's select only cities beginning with the letter *B*, then, from that list, show invoices with totals averaging more than five (Figure 110).

```
SELECT
    BillingCity,
    AVG(Total)
FROM
    invoices
WHERE
    BillingCity LIKE 'B%'
GROUP BY
    BillingCity
HAVING
    AVG(Total) > 5
ORDER BY
    BillingCity
```

In this query we performed the same task, but this time we added a WHERE clause to filter results to only cities starting with *B*. This filtering step is performed before the HAVING and ORDER BY clauses are processed. Since we must filter before we can group, the order of these filtering clauses is important, and WHERE most always comes before HAVING.

	BillingCity	AVG(Total)
1	Bangalore	6.106666667
2	Berlin	5.374285714
3	Bordeaux	5.66
4	Boston	5.374285714
5	Brasília	5.374285714
6	Brussels	5.374285714
7	Budapest	6.517142857
8	Buenos Aires	5.374285714
	8 rows returned in 1ms	

Using GROUP BY with Multiple Fields

It is possible to group by more than one aggregate field at a time. Let's say we want a more detailed breakdown of average invoices. We can write our query so that our aggregate data is grouped first by country and then by city. In the example below, we add another field, BillingCountry, to our GROUP BY clause. Let's see how our query functions.

```
SELECT
    BillingCountry,
    BillingCity,
    AVG(Total)
FROM
    invoices
GROUP BY
    BillingCountry, BillingCity
ORDER BY
    BillingCountry
```

As we can see in our result set (Figure 111), we have multiple entries for the same billing country, with the individual cities listed in the adjacent column. Grouping by multiple fields can be very useful when we desire a more detailed breakdown of information.

REMEMBER

Database files are likely to contain spelling and/or capitalization errors.

	BillingCountry	BillingCity	AVG(Total)
1	Argentina	Buenos Aires	5.374285714
2	Australia	Sidney	5.374285714
3	Austria	Sidney	6.088571429
4	Belgium	Brussels	5.374285714
5	Brazil	Brasília	5.374285714
6	Brazil	Rio de Janeiro	5.374285714
7	Brazil	São José dos Campos	5.66
8	Brazil	São Paulo	5.374285714
9	Canada	Edmonton	5.374285714
10	Canada	Halifax	5.374285714
...	53 rows returned in 6ms		

GRAPHIC

fig. 111

A Final Word on Functions

This section is by no means exhaustive, but hopefully it showed you the power of functions and their ability to turn data into information and answer real-world questions. If we were to go over all the functions in SQLite and give an example of each, we would have to provide a carrying device for this book with some sturdy wheels. Fortunately, there is a wealth of information online about SQL functions and their use. I often encourage students, in addition to using the SQLite documentation website referred to in this chapter, to perform a web search for functions to see what other people have done with them. Hopefully this chapter has sparked your interest and you can continue your learning journey on your own and discover even more ways to use these powerful tools.

Data Analysis Checkpoint

1. Create a single-line mailing list for all US customers, including capitalized full names and full addresses with five-digit zip codes, in the following format:

   FRANK HARRIS 1600 Amphitheatre Parkway, Mountain View, CA 94043

2. What are the average annual sales generated by customers from the USA from all years of data available?

3. What are the company's all-time total sales?

4. Who are the top ten best customers from a revenue standpoint? *Hint:* you will need to use a join (chapter 6) to answer this question.

Chapter Recap

» Functions allow you to alter, reformat, and perform calculations on the data in your tables.

» Queries containing numerical data can be manipulated with a variety of arithmetic operations and aggregate functions.

» Queries containing text can be split, concatenated, capitalized, etc.

» Once data is aggregated with functions, it can be further sorted by the GROUP BY and HAVING clauses.

» The HAVING clause does for aggregate fields what the WHERE clause does for non-aggregate fields.

» The HAVING clause can be used in a query only if a GROUP BY clause is also present.

» You can use GROUP BY with multiple fields to further narrow down your aggregated data.

PART III

MORE ADVANCED SQL TOPICS

| 8 |
Subqueries

A subquery is simply one query nested inside of another query, usually in the SELECT, FROM or WHERE clause. Subqueries are useful when the query we want to create requires a few additional steps or calculations to produce the dataset we desire. For example, subqueries are very helpful for scenarios where we want to view or compare a query by a condition that requires its own query to calculate. Instead of writing one query, then copying the results into the next query, we can use a subquery that performs both operations at once. Subqueries also provide us with another method of simultaneously accessing data from more than one table. Although a subquery is not as powerful as a join, it can help us perform a calculation in one table and then use that calculation in conjunction with another table. Let's begin our exploration of subqueries by looking at their use with aggregate functions.

Introduction to Subqueries Using Aggregate Functions

To illustrate the use of subqueries, we will begin with a simple SELECT statement that we used in the last chapter to return the average invoice total from the invoices table:

```
SELECT
    ROUND(AVG(Total), 2) AS [Average Total]
FROM
    invoices
```

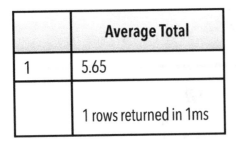

	Average Total
1	5.65
	1 rows returned in 1ms

fig. 112

We add the ROUND() function to round the AVG() function to two significant figures.

We can see that our sample query gives us an average invoice value of $5.65 from the *invoices* table. Let's say we were asked by our sTunes company to gather data about all invoices that were lower than this average. First, we need a SELECT statement that displays some of the invoice fields (such as InvoiceDate, BillingAddress, BillingCity, and, of course, Total). We would then want to filter our results by comparing them to an aggregate function. We want a WHERE clause that compares Total to AVG(Total). We learned in the last chapter that attempting a direct comparison within the WHERE clause using a statement such as WHERE Total < AVG(Total) would be incorrect and cause a "misuse of aggregate function" error. So we need a way to take the entire query listed above and insert all of it inside another query that sorts invoices by total. Fortunately, there is an easy way to accomplish this.

We start by writing a basic SELECT statement and then inserting the entire query above into our WHERE clause using parentheses (), making it function as a subquery.

```
SELECT
    InvoiceDate,
    BillingAddress,
    BillingCity,
    Total
FROM
    invoices
```

```
WHERE Total <
(select
    AVG(Total)
from
    invoices)
ORDER BY
    Total DESC
```

The query that we surround with parentheses is called the *inner query*, which will become part of the WHERE clause of our *outer query*.

fig. 113

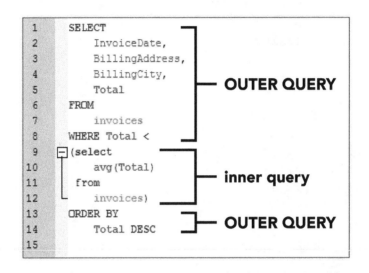

MY TAKE

In Figure 113, we capitalized our SELECT statement and other operators in our outer query, but our statements and functions inside of our inner query are all in lowercase. There is no universal rule about whether your operators or functions should be capitalized or not. The RDBMS doesn't mind either way. I personally find that using capital letters for outer query operators and functions and lowercase letters for subqueries increases readability. It helps to visually differentiate between the outer and inner query statements.

Using a Subquery in the SELECT Statement

If the items in our select statement require an additional step (such as an aggregate calculation), then we will need a subquery to perform that calculation. In the last chapter on functions, we used the GROUP BY statement to show average subtotals of invoices by city. What if we were asked by our sTunes company how each individual city was performing against global average sales? One way to answer that question would be to write a query that was able to display the average sales of each city right next to the global average.

The query we write to display the average sales by BillingCity is identical to the one we wrote in the previous chapter, with one exception. We also include a subquery in the SELECT clause to calculate the global average. This way we can compare the two values.

```
SELECT
    BillingCity,
    AVG(Total) AS [City Average],
    (select
            avg(total)
    from
            invoices) AS [Global Average]
FROM
    invoices
GROUP BY
    BillingCity
ORDER BY
    BillingCity
```

Running this query shows how each city performs against the global average.

fig. 114

	BillingCity	City Average	Global Average
1	Amsterdam	5.802857143	5.651941748
2	Bangalore	6.106666667	5.651941748
3	Berlin	5.374285714	5.651941748
4	Bordeaux	5.66	5.651941748
5	Boston	5.374285714	5.651941748
...	53 rows returned in 5ms		

You can see from this output that the numerical value for "Global Average" remains the same in each record returned, making it easy for us to compare the average invoice totals by city against the global average.

ON YOUR OWN:
» Modify this query with the ROUND() function to display only two decimal points.

Using a WHERE Clause in a Subquery

There will be times when we want to have a more detailed query function as our subquery. Our outer query can have a WHERE clause which, in turn, contains a subquery with its own WHERE clause. A good example of when we would want a WHERE clause in a subquery is when we want to compare all fields to a specific instance. Let's say that we were asked to find the all-time largest sale from our dataset (2009–2012) and to see if there are any invoice totals in the latest year of records (2013) that are higher than that value. To answer this question, we would first have to get the largest sale prior to 2013. We can do that with the MAX() function.

```
SELECT
    MAX(Total)
FROM
    invoices
WHERE
    InvoiceDate < '2013-01-01'
```

fig. 115

	MAX(Total)
1	23.86
	1 rows returned in 1ms

Now that we know this value, we wrap this query in parentheses () and then write our outer query and include the additional fields that we need.

```
SELECT
    InvoiceDate,
    BillingCity,
    Total
FROM
    invoices
WHERE
    InvoiceDate >= '2013-01-01' AND total >
    (select
        max(Total)
    from
        invoices
    where
        InvoiceDate < '2013-01-01')
```

We can see from this query that we broke our record for highest invoice total on November 13, 2013.

fig. 116

	InvoiceDate	BillingCity	Total
1	2013-11-13 00:00:00	Prague	25.86
	1 rows returned in 2ms		

ON YOUR OWN:

» How many invoices were recorded on or before January 1, 2010, that were above the average invoice amount?

Subqueries without Aggregate Functions

A subquery does not always contain an aggregate function. The following query shows the transaction date for a specific transaction.

```
SELECT
    InvoiceDate
FROM
    invoices
WHERE
    InvoiceId = 251
```

fig. 117

	InvoiceDate
1	2012-01-09 00:00:00
	1 rows returned in 1ms

If we wanted to see if there were any other invoices that were received after the invoice referenced above, we would build a subquery wrapped in a pair of parentheses and then build an outer query around it.

```
SELECT
    InvoiceDate,
    BillingAddress,
    BillingCity
FROM
    invoices
```

```
WHERE
    InvoiceDate >
(select
    InvoiceDate
from
    invoices
where
    InvoiceId = 251)
```

GRAPHIC

fig. 118

	InvoiceDate	BillingAddress	BillingCity
1	2012-01-22 00:00:00	Av. Paulista, 2022	São Paulo
2	2012-01-22 00:00:00	Qe 7 Bloco G	Brasília
3	2012-01-23 00:00:00	700 W Pender Street	Vancouver
4	2012-01-24 00:00:00	1 Infinite Loop	Cupertino
5	2012-01-27 00:00:00	319 N. Frances Street	Madison
...	161 rows returned in 8ms		

Returning Multiple Values from a Subquery

Up to this point we have only used subqueries to calculate a singular value, which is then passed to the outer query. It is possible to use subqueries that return multiple records. Let's say our sTunes management is interested in three particular invoices. To select those three invoices, consider the following query.

```
SELECT
    InvoiceDate
FROM
    invoices
WHERE
    InvoiceId IN (251, 252, 255)
```

GRAPHIC

fig. 119

	InvoiceDate
1	2012-01-09 00:00:00
2	2012-01-22 00:00:00
3	2012-01-24 00:00:00
...	3 rows returned in 1ms

The preceding query uses the IN clause to return three dates from the *invoices* table: 2012-01-09, 2012-01-22, and 2012-01-24. Now let's say we are asked if any other purchases were made on those three days. If we want to select all invoices for those three days, we can start a new query, or just use our previous query as a subquery, like this:

```
SELECT
    InvoiceDate,
    BillingAddress,
    BillingCity
FROM
    invoices
WHERE
    InvoiceDate IN
(select
    InvoiceDate
from
    invoices
where
    InvoiceId in (251, 252, 255))
```

GRAPHIC

fig. 120

	InvoiceDate	BillingAddress	BillingCity
1	2012-01-09 00:00:00	Rua Dr. Falcão Filho, 155	São Paulo
2	2012-01-22 00:00:00	Av. Paulista, 2022	São Paulo
3	2012-01-22 00:00:00	Qe 7 Bloco G	Brasília
4	2012-01-24 00:00:00	1 Infinite Loop	Cupertino
...	4 rows returned in 2ms		

The technique of turning an existing query into a subquery is useful when you are "dialing in" on your data. This method allows you to reuse an existing query and modify it to further narrow down your search.

Subqueries and the DISTINCT Clause

As we have seen from the other examples in this chapter, subqueries are very helpful for scenarios where you want to view or compare a query by a condition that requires its own query to calculate. As we learned in chapter 1, there is usually one unique field in every table known as the primary key that contains a unique number for every record, but other fields can have redundant information. To work better with redundant information, it is often convenient to filter this data so that it only displays unique, or distinct, values. This is where the DISTINCT keyword comes in. To demonstrate subqueries and the DISTINCT keyword, let's look at the *tracks* and *invoice_items* tables.

The *invoice_items* table shows us which individual sTunes tracks were purchased on each invoice. If we create a query that shows us the InvoiceId and TrackId fields ordered by TrackId, we can see that certain track numbers were ordered multiple times across different invoices.

```
SELECT
    InvoiceId,
    TrackId
FROM
    invoice_items
ORDER BY
    TrackId
```

fig. 121

	InvoiceId	TrackId
1	108	1
2	1	2
3	214	2
4	319	3
5	1	4
6	108	5
7	2	6
8	2	8
9	214	8
10	108	9
...	2240 rows returned in 15ms	

For example, we can see that tracks #2 and #8 appear on multiple invoices, meaning they were ordered multiple times (Figure 121). However, track #7 does not appear to have an invoice available, so we can infer that no one in our record set has purchased it. Our sTunes management is interested in discovering which tracks are not selling. We would need to find a table that links TrackId with InvoiceId. We could use subqueries to list all tracks (by composer and name) that don't appear in the *invoice_items* table.

fig. 122

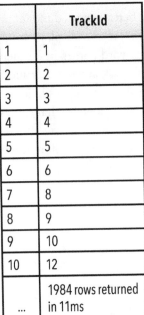
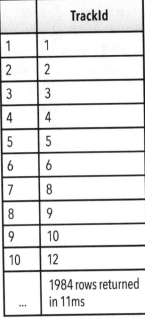

	TrackId
1	1
2	2
3	3
4	4
5	5
6	6
7	8
8	9
9	10
10	12
...	1984 rows returned in 11ms

If we run the same query again, this time with the keyword DISTINCT, we will get a list of only those tracks that appear on invoices without any of the duplicates.

```
SELECT
    DISTINCT TrackId
FROM
    invoice_items
ORDER BY
    TrackId
```

We can see again that some TrackId numbers (such as #7) do not appear in any invoices, but all the listings of tracks that appear on multiple invoices are reduced to just one instance. Now we need a query that lists all tracks from our *tracks* table that are NOT IN the list created by our first query.

```
SELECT
    TrackId,
    Composer,
    Name
FROM
    tracks
WHERE
    TrackId NOT IN
            (select distinct
                    TrackId
            from
                    invoice_items)
```

We now have a list of songs that didn't appear on any invoice (Figure 123). Looking at our results, we can see that the track we identified previously, track #7, is at the very top of the list of tracks that did not sell. Now our sTunes sales team has a clear picture of what songs have not been purchased.

The examples of subqueries given in this chapter are obviously not exhaustive. There are many more ways to use subqueries, but all the examples given share a common theme. Subqueries can make complex multistep calculations achievable with just one query. They allow you to calculate a specific condition and then compare a new set of data against that same condition.

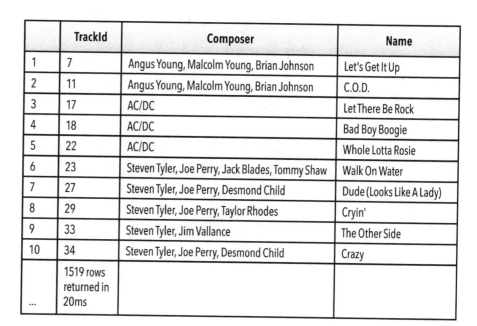

	TrackId	Composer	Name
1	7	Angus Young, Malcolm Young, Brian Johnson	Let's Get It Up
2	11	Angus Young, Malcolm Young, Brian Johnson	C.O.D.
3	17	AC/DC	Let There Be Rock
4	18	AC/DC	Bad Boy Boogie
5	22	AC/DC	Whole Lotta Rosie
6	23	Steven Tyler, Joe Perry, Jack Blades, Tommy Shaw	Walk On Water
7	27	Steven Tyler, Joe Perry, Desmond Child	Dude (Looks Like A Lady)
8	29	Steven Tyler, Joe Perry, Taylor Rhodes	Cryin'
9	33	Steven Tyler, Jim Vallance	The Other Side
10	34	Steven Tyler, Joe Perry, Desmond Child	Crazy
...	1519 rows returned in 20ms		

GRAPHIC

fig. 123

NOTE

Subqueries give us another quick way of interacting between tables that have key fields in common. If we were doing extensive work with both tables, it would be better to create a join between the `TrackId` and the *tracks* table (instead of using subqueries) so we could display all the information side by side.

Data Analysis Checkpoint

1. How many invoices exceed the average invoice amount generated in 2010?

2. Who are the customers responsible for these invoices?

3. How many of these customers are from the USA?

Chapter Recap

» Subqueries allow you to execute multiple SQL statements within a single query.

» Subqueries are comprised of two or more separate SQL statements identified as inner and outer queries.

» Subqueries are usually used to compare existing data with data you derive with aggregates or other functions.

» The DISTINCT keyword allows you to ignore redundant data in records and search for unique instances only.

191
Views

Chapter Overview
- » Creating views
- » Modifying existing views
- » Views and joins
- » Removing views
- » Data Analysis Checkpoint

A view is referred to as a virtual table. It is simply an SQL query that is saved and can be executed repeatedly or referenced (as a subquery) by other queries. Views are helpful when you find yourself repeatedly constructing the same query, especially if the query is complex or difficult to write. In our operation scenario, if sTunes company management asks us for the same sales data every week or quarter, we might want to prepare a view with that information precalculated. Let's examine the many ways we can incorporate views into our existing SQL knowledge.

Turning Previous Queries into Views
The SQL statements we have introduced in previous chapters can all be saved and reused when we create a view out of them. Let's take a look at the query featured in the beginning of chapter 8.

```
SELECT
    ROUND(AVG(Total), 2) AS [Average Total]
FROM
    invoices
```

We can turn this statement into a view by adding CREATE VIEW V_ AvgTotal AS above the top line of the query:

```
CREATE VIEW V_AvgTotal AS
SELECT
    ROUND(AVG(Total), 2) AS [Average Total]
FROM
    invoices
```

We have now created a view called `V_AvgTotal`.

Naming views beginning with `V_` is a useful naming convention because it lets anyone reading our code know that they are dealing with a view. After the underscore symbol, we include a brief description of how the view functions, using further underscores if needed. We could also name this view `V_AvgTotal_Rounded`. Choose whatever makes the most sense to you.

When we execute this statement, we get a message that says "`Query executed successfully: CREATE VIEW V_AvgTotal AS.`" If we then look in our Database Structure tab in DB Browser, the view `V_AvgTotal` can be observed under a section called Views.

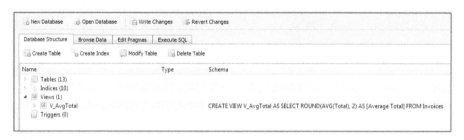

fig. 124

Now that this view is created, there are some simple tasks we can perform just by right-clicking on it. When we right-click on the view, we get the following menu box (Figure 125):

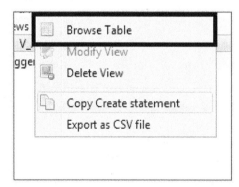

fig. 125

Selecting the "Browse Table" option will move us to the adjacent Browse Data tab where we can investigate the contents of our view, as we would with any table in the database. From this menu, we can also delete the view or generate a copy of the code (which we typed earlier) that created it.

Figure 125 shows a "Modify View" option that (at the time of publication) is grayed out and inaccessible. Modifying existing views is not a feature supported by the version of DB Browser we are currently using. However, in other implementations of SQL, such as SQL Server, it is possible to modify existing views. We will explain how to modify a view in SQLite later in this chapter.

Why We Use Views

Views are helpful for a number of reasons, but convenience is definitely the main one. If you find yourself repeatedly writing the same query, or continually referring to a particular join that shows how two tables interact together, it may be convenient to save that query as a view so that it can be referenced when you need it. Also, when a query is saved as a view, it can be called up as a subquery by selecting the view name.

Let's refer back to the view V_AvgTotal that we created at the beginning of this chapter. You may remember from chapter 8 that we used the average function as a subquery so that we could compare the totals of invoices against the average total of all invoices. Instead of writing out the full average subquery in our statement, we could write our query this way instead:

```
SELECT
    InvoiceDate,
    BillingAddress,
    BillingCity,
    Total
FROM
    invoices
WHERE Total <
    (select
            *
    from
            V_AvgTotal)
ORDER BY
    Total DESC
```

Even though our view is a complete SQL statement, we still need to reference it in a SELECT statement when using it with subqueries. We use the * symbol in SELECT statements to get views to return all rows from the view being referenced. In this case, there is only one row, which is our aggregate sum. This allows us to select only parts of a view.

If any query is one we frequently use as a subquery, then establishing it as a view allows us to simplify our code and make what we are doing more transparent. If anyone (a coworker, for example) wants to look under the hood, they can simply navigate to the Database Structure tab and investigate how our views function. Using views cuts down on creation time, especially as our queries get longer and more advanced.

How to Modify a View

As we mentioned earlier, the current iteration of DB Browser (at the time of this writing) does not support modifying existing views. As a workaround in SQLite, we would need to create a new view and give it a new name, or delete the existing view. To modify a view in SQLite, we would navigate to the Database Structure tab, right-click on the view, and copy the CREATE VIEW statement. We could then paste the results into our Execute SQL tab, make our modifications, and run the statement again.

NOTE

When re-running your view, if you still have the original view saved in the Views section, you will have to rename your new view (or remove the existing view) or else you will get an error telling you that your view already exists. All views need unique names.

ON YOUR OWN:

»   Modify the V_AvgTotal view to remove the ROUND() function.
»   Pick a different subquery example from chapter 8, turn the subquery portion into a view, and run it again.

Creating a View from Joins

Views are very good for storing longer or more involved queries. In chapter 6, we learned about joins. Joins are excellent candidates to add as views because they help us visualize the relationships between tables and they also can be very extensive queries that we might want to save instead of typing again. In the last chapter on subqueries, we used the *invoice_items* table and the *tracks* table together to find out which songs from our *tracks* table had never been ordered. It would have been helpful to have a view linking those two tables together that we could have either referenced in our subquery or just saved as a view to refer to when needed.

To create a view for these two tables, we first need to decide what kind of join we want to use. Since we are looking for correlating fields, we will use an INNER JOIN on *tracks* and *invoice_items*.

```
SELECT
    ii.InvoiceId,
    ii.UnitPrice,
    ii.Quantity,
    t.Name,
    t.Composer,
    t.Milliseconds
FROM
    invoice_items ii
INNER JOIN
    tracks t
ON ii.TrackId = t.TrackId
```

When we create joins, we use short aliases for each table involved and then relate the tables to each other using a common field. We use t for *tracks* and ii for *invoice_items* since we are already using i for the *invoices* table.

Now that we have our join, we can add one more line at the beginning of the query to save it as a view.

```
CREATE VIEW V_Tracks_InvoiceItems AS
SELECT
    ii.InvoiceId,
    ii.UnitPrice,
    ii.Quantity,
    t.Name,
    t.Composer,
    t.Milliseconds
FROM
    invoice_items ii
INNER JOIN
    tracks t
ON ii.TrackId = t.TrackId
```

Next, we are going to take an existing join from chapter 6, one that merges the *invoices*, *customers*, and *employees* tables, and save that as a view as well.

```
CREATE VIEW V_inv_cus_emp AS
SELECT
    i.InvoiceId,
    i.InvoiceDate,
    i.Total,
    i.CustomerId,
    c.FirstName,
    c.LastName,
    c.SupportRepId,
    e.EmployeeId,
    e.LastName,
    e.FirstName,
    e.Title
FROM
    invoices AS i
INNER JOIN
    customers AS c
ON
    i.CustomerId = c.CustomerId
INNER JOIN
    employees AS e
ON
    e.EmployeeId = c.SupportRepId
ORDER BY
    InvoiceDate
```

We have made a slight modification from the way this join was presented in chapter 6. We have removed the * symbol from the `SELECT` statement. The point of views is to show just what you need. So we have included only the relevant fields from *invoices*, *customers*, and *employees*.

We can see that we have both of these joins saved as views in our Database Structure tab (Figure 126).

fig. 126

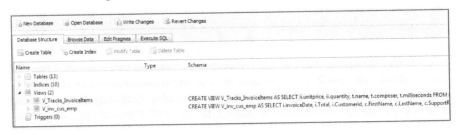

Now that we have these two joins saved as views, we use both of them in an inner join:

```
SELECT *
FROM
    V_Tracks_InvoiceItems ii
INNER JOIN
    V_inv_cus_emp ice
ON
    ii.InvoiceId = ice.InvoiceId
```

With the above query joining five tables together, we can now know what tracks were sold by each employee and which customer they were sold to. By aggregating the data, we can also determine which track was sold the most, how much total revenue was generated by the track, and the employee responsible for each sale. We can now go even further and save our aggregation as a view if we want to.

Joins between multiple views will only work if the key fields held in common from all of these tables were included in the initial join.

Removing a View Using the DROP Statement

Although we have shown that you can remove a view by right-clicking on the view name in the Database Structure tab, a view can also be removed by using a statement called the DROP clause. To use this command, we type the following:

```
DROP VIEW
    V_AvgTotal
```

The previous statement will delete the V_AvgTotal view. Only the view is removed from the database—no data is affected by using the DROP VIEW syntax.

If you remove a view that is referenced by other views, those views will not function anymore.

The DROP command is a command to remove elements. It can also remove your tables. See the next chapter for best practices concerning tools that edit or remove data permanently. As mentioned earlier, a view can also be removed from your database by right-clicking on it and selecting "Remove View."

Data Analysis Checkpoint

For this checkpoint, we will be using a query from chapter 8: Using a Subquery in the SELECT Statement. We have reproduced it here:

```
SELECT
    BillingCity,
    AVG(Total) AS [City Average],
    (select
        avg(total)
    from
        invoices) AS [Global Average]
FROM
    invoices
GROUP BY
    BillingCity
ORDER BY
    BillingCity
```

1. Take the inner query (by itself) from this SELECT statement and create a view from it. Save the view as V_GlobalAverage.

2. Remove the subquery from the above code entirely and substitute it for your newly created view V_GlobalAverage.

3. Save this new query as a view called V_CityAvgVsGlobalAvg.

4. Delete the view V_GlobalAverage. What happens to V_CityAvgVsGlobalAvg?

Chapter Recap

» Views are virtual queries created with SQL that can be selected by other queries.

» Views are created by adding `CREATE VIEW V_VIEWNAME AS` at the beginning of a query.

» View are particularly useful for long queries that may be used or referred to frequently.

» Views can be modified and deleted by using features from your RDBMS implementation or by using SQL commands.

| 10 |
Data Manipulation Language (DML)

Chapter Overview
- » Caution
- » The role of DML
- » Inserting data
- » Updating data
- » Deleting data
- » Data Analysis Checkpoint

All SQL statements we have presented so far have been used in a way that either retrieves data from the database or creates derived data based on existing database values. This chapter introduces *data manipulation language (DML)* and examines SQL statements that are used to change or alter the data that is stored in the tables of a database.

It is best to practice these commands in a sandbox space, such as the sample database provided. Using DML on a live database with active customer data could have permanent deleterious effects.

Data Analysis Versus Database Management

Throughout this book so far, the primary purpose of our SQL queries was to take existing data in our database and turn it into actionable information that would be useful to the fictional stakeholders at our sTunes company. But as we mentioned in the introduction, the functions of SQL far exceed the task of turning data into meaningful information. There are roles such as database developer and database administrator that oversee the growth, improvement, and management of the company database. The extent and scope of these roles differ from company to company and from one database implementation to another. Even among experienced SQL users, there are differing opinions about whether DML is a separate field of study or if it should be learned in tandem with SQL statements designed to extract information only.

The different database roles can be a point of confusion for beginners. DML fits neatly into the category of database administration and development, but in a smaller company employing just one database, the roles of data analyst, developer, and administrator may all be assigned to one person, and that person might be you! So even if your main goal is just to learn how to write useful select queries, it is valuable at the very least to understand how DML works.

For the purpose of this chapter, statements that are referred to as data manipulation language (DML) are INSERT, UPDATE, and DELETE. As the names imply, these statements can be used to add, modify, and remove data from the tables in your database. For our sTunes operational scenario, we will demonstrate how we would handle a request from sTunes management to add additional artists to our existing music offerings, add new records, and then delete those records.

In DB Browser, making any changes to the sTunes database using DML will prompt the program to ask if you want to save your changes when you exit the program or close the database file. You can make a copy of the original database file so that you can practice these modifications, save them, and still retain the original.

Inserting Data into a Database

The INSERT statement is used to insert data into a table one row at a time. There are a couple of ways to compose an INSERT statement. One way is using INSERT INTO and specifying the desired field. Let's say our sTunes company is expanding their music selection and wants us to add some additional artists to the *artists* table.

The following INSERT statement will insert a new record into the *artists* table.

```
INSERT INTO
artists (Name)
VALUES ('Bob Marley')
```

There are three elements to this insertion: a table, a field, and a value. The table *artists* is specified after the keywords INSERT INTO. This identifies which table we want to modify. This is followed by the field name surrounded by parentheses (). In this case, we want to add a new artist by adding the artist's name to the Name field. This is then followed by the keyword VALUES, where opening and closing parentheses surround the actual value that is being inserted into the *artists* table. In this example, the value is Bob Marley. "Bob Marley" is a text value, so it is also surrounded by single quotes.

We can check on the data type of the Name field in the *artists* table by looking at our Database Structure tab. We notice that the data type is NVARCHAR(120), which is a character data type with an expected limit of 120 characters.

ON YOUR OWN:
» What is the result of running the INSERT statement above?
» Write a SELECT statement to find the newly inserted value.
» Insert the value "Peter Tosh" into the *artists* table.
» What is the ArtistId value for the newly added Bob Marley record?

There is a second column in the *artists* table called ArtistId. This column did not need to be specified in the INSERT statement because it is an Auto Increment column. This means that a new number is automatically created in the column for new records that are added.

Another way to insert values into a table is to list the values sequentially by field name. If you insert data in this way, you do not have to specify the columns in which data is to be stored. However, when composing an INSERT statement in this manner, special care must be taken to ensure that the order in which data is specified in the INSERT statement is the same order in which the target fields exist in the table.

The following INSERT statement will also insert a new record into the *employees* table:

```
INSERT INTO
employees
VALUES ('9', 'Martin', 'Ricky', 'Sales Support
Agent', '2', '1975-02-07', '2018-01-05', '123 Houston
St', 'New York', 'NY', 'United States', '11201', '(347)
525-8588', '', 'rmartin@gmail.com')
```

As mentioned earlier, special care must be taken to ensure the order in which data is specified in the INSERT statement matches the order of the fields in the target table. So as a precaution it is a good practice to examine the target table and take note of the order in which the fields appear.

fig. 127

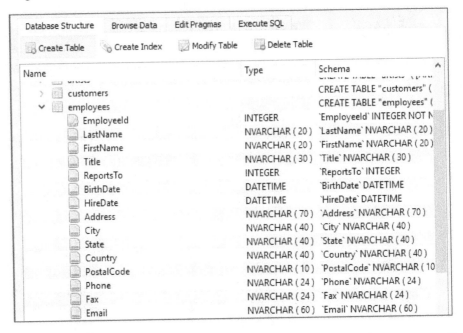

By checking the Database Structure tab, we can observe the structure of the *employees* table. The layout of the fields from EmployeeId thru Email must be specified in this exact order when using the INSERT statement that was last introduced.

ON YOUR OWN:

» What is the result of the INSERT statement when executed?
» The newly entered employee, Ricky Martin, does not have a fax number; how is this expressed in the INSERT statement?
» Insert another employee record into the *employees* table.
» Run the query again, but use an existing primary key. What error message do you get?

When inserting records where no value exists for a field, you still need to include a pair of empty quote marks ' ' for the value that does not exist. In the example above, we omitted the fax number by placing a pair of empty quotes in the same position that the fax number field appears in the *employees* table.

Updating Data and the SET Keyword

The UPDATE statement is used to modify existing data in a table. It is generally used with the WHERE clause. The WHERE clause is used with the UPDATE statement to specify the particular rows of data you intend to update. Without the WHERE clause, an UPDATE statement will update all rows contained in a table.

The following statement updates the employee record we inserted in the previous section.

```
UPDATE
employees
SET PostalCode = '11202'
WHERE
    EmployeeId = 9
```

If you haven't added any employees yet, running this code will give you a "No Such Column" error.

In the previous syntax, the *employees* table is specified after the keyword UPDATE. Next comes the keyword SET, and this is where you specify the column within the *employees* table that you intend to update; in our example it is the PostalCode field. This is followed by an equals sign (=) and the new value we intend to update the old value to. In our example this value is '11202' (surrounded with single quotes because zip code is a string value). Following the SET keyword is the WHERE clause, which allows us to specify exactly which employee record we intend to update. By specifying EmployeeId = 9 we ensure that only this employee record is updated and no other.

ON YOUR OWN:

» What is the result of the UPDATE statement in our example above?
» Compose another UPDATE statement and change the phone number for Ricky Martin.
» How many rows would be affected by our UPDATE statement if it didn't include a WHERE clause?

Particular importance must be paid to the inclusion of the WHERE clause in UPDATE statements. Without ensuring that a WHERE clause is included and is specifying the intended record modification, you can update records you didn't intend to, which can have significant adverse effects.

Instead of executing an UPDATE statement right away, first compose a SELECT statement using the same table and WHERE clause; this way you can preview what you are about to update. Once the SELECT statement returns the expected records, you can then execute your UPDATE statement.

Deleting Data

The DELETE statement is used to remove existing records from a table. This statement, like UPDATE, is generally used with the WHERE clause. Without the WHERE clause, a DELETE statement will delete all rows contained in a table.

As we did with UPDATE, instead of executing a DELETE statement right away, first compose a SELECT statement using the same table(s) and a WHERE clause; this way you can preview what you are about to delete. Once the select statement returns the expected records, you can then execute your DELETE statement.

First, we create a SELECT statement to verify the data we are about to remove.

```
SELECT * FROM
    employees
WHERE
    EmployeeId = 9
```

Once we are sure we want to remove this data, the following statement deletes the employee record we updated in the previous section.

```
DELETE FROM
    employees
WHERE
    EmployeeId = 9
```

The above DELETE statement begins with two keywords, DELETE FROM, which is followed by the name of the table we intend to delete a record from. In our example, we are deleting a record from our *employees* table. Following the table name is the WHERE clause, which allows us to specify exactly which employee record we intend to delete. By specifying EmployeeId = 9 we ensure that only this employee record is deleted and no other.

ON YOUR OWN:

» What is the result of the DELETE statement above, when executed?

» Compose another DELETE statement and remove all employees who are sales support agents.

» How many records were affected by the DELETE statement you composed in the previous question?

Particular importance must be paid to the inclusion of the WHERE clause in DELETE statements. Without ensuring that a WHERE clause is included and is specifying the record(s) intended for deletion, you can delete records you didn't intend to, which can have significant adverse effects.

Data Analysis Checkpoint

1. Add a new customer to the database.

2. Create an invoice record for this customer.

3. Remove this customer from the database.

Chapter Recap

» The statements in this chapter can permanently alter database data. Check carefully that this is your intention before using these statements.

» DML refers to the collection of clauses (INSERT, UPDATE, and DELETE) capable of creating and manipulating existing data in a database.

» The INSERT statement is used to add new records to a database.

» The UPDATE statement can modify existing records and change the values.

» The DELETE statement removes records entirely.

Conclusion

It Is All About Asking Good Questions

If you have made it this far, you have seen how we can use Structured Query Language to turn lifeless entries in a database into meaningful information that you or your company can use to make the tough decisions that define every business venture. Throughout this book, I have tried to demonstrate how to write efficient but intelligent queries using real-world scenarios that showcase the methods that I myself have found useful and still use today. I have tried my best to avoid the philosophical debates, technicalities, and academic jargon that plague every body of technical knowledge in order to bring you by the purest and most expedient path to your own unique mastery of SQL. To the beginner: I hope you have enjoyed this journey we have taken together and that I have built a bridge for you to continue on your path to data mastery. To those with previous experience: I hope this book has highlighted a few insights and given you a sandbox to test your ever-growing SQL toolbox. In closing, I would like to share a few more practical insights and lessons I have learned over my eighteen years of working in the industry of information. It is my hope that the principles I've distilled from both the successes and mistakes I've made over the years will help steer you in the right direction when it comes to pursuing your next step of SQL mastery. In this section I will address some of the questions my students frequently ask me and talk briefly about further SQL education and certifications.

Finding Your Niche

It is my hope that, throughout the course of this book, you have seen a wide variety of different applications of SQL. Some may interest you and others may not. Computer science was a very wide field when I started my own journey into the world of data eighteen years ago. At the time, I was working with Visual Basic and building applications; in other words, the front end, or visual interface, of software systems. Eventually I had to incorporate databases into these applications. Once I started working with Microsoft Access and experienced the way it helped me visualize data and how the tables were connected, it really opened my eyes to how data works and deepened my understanding of databases. As I gained more experience,

I realized that data was the backbone of my work. Understanding the world of big data became an obsession for me. This might happen to you—in fact, I hope it does. I encourage my students to branch out to as many related programming disciplines as they may run into in their careers. The specialty that fits you the best may be one good question away! Your path is never a straight line. All the struggles, errors, and blunders along the way will help clarify what you find worthwhile.

Choosing the Right Database Occupation

Although we have focused mainly on the role of the database analyst (using your skills in query composition, composing statements, and answering everyday questions), there is plenty of demand for database designers as well. If you have ever wondered who decides what fields will be contained in any given table, or how the tables will relate to each other, that is the job of a database designer/modeler. For example, in chapter 6 we introduced the concept of normalization, which is the prevention of data redundancy in multiple tables. Database management also deals with access restrictions, backups, and disaster recovery. These topics are beyond the scope of this book. If you find yourself curious to know more about how databases are made and maintained, then you may want to look more into database design as a career.

Is It All about the Money?

Often when I am having discussions with students about careers in data, they ask me some form of this question: "Which particular database occupation or niche field is going to make me the most money?" Since I began teaching people in coffee shops, I've encountered a lot of people who are motivated by money. This is not a bad thing. It is a reasonable starting point, but not the big picture. Any occupation that pays well is going to take a lot of time and sacrifice. There are plenty of opportunities for people chasing the highest dollar.

However, as my own personal experience has taught me, there are going to be several moments, perhaps late at night when you're surrounded by empty coffee cups, when you are going to ask yourself, "Is this what I really wanted to do? Is this even worth it?" There will be moments, many of them, when you are pushed to your limits and you are going to question your decision about taking that job or career path, if your only motivation was money. Through trial and plenty of error, I've discovered that what pushes me through those rough moments has been ensuring that I can always link my current task with the passion for learning that brought me to this industry in the first place. In my own career path, I've found that helping others—more specifically, seeing my students' faces light up as they reach that learning epiphany—gives me more satisfaction than the oftentimes repetitive nature of the corporate environment. Starting my own business and helping people directly, helping them feed that natural desire to learn, was much more fulfilling for me. But that was my experience. Your own path will be unique to you.

Instead of just chasing the highest payout, I suggest you remind yourself, daily if necessary, of what drew your interest to this occupation in the first place. In other words, the more important question is what particular database occupation or niche field excites you or gives you the opportunity to create? There is a way to monetize your passions. The scope of this industry is comprehensive, so whether your interest is in medicine, sports, travel, or governmental policy, there will be a data analysis occupation waiting for you in any of those fields.

Is SQL Knowledge Universal?

"What do I need to know before using my skills with a different SQL implementation?" I encounter this question frequently from students looking for a specific job opportunity. Perhaps the job application states that experience in a specific SQL implementation, such as SQL Server, is required. Although there are key differences in every database implementation, I encourage my students not to be discouraged or in any way deterred by requests for specific implementation knowledge. The core principles you have learned in this book will assist you no matter what database system you eventually find yourself working on. The beauty of SQL is that it is the universal language of data. If you find yourself working on a database implementation that isn't SQLite, do not worry. Every implementation will have the same basic attributes you have learned in this book. Whatever the vendor, there will be an SQL pane to enter queries, a button to run statements, a place that gives you feedback on your query and how long it took to process. The result you receive will always be presented in columns and rows. The relational database structure you learned about in chapter 1 is an industry standard, and the database will be organized and normalized very similarly whether you are working with Oracle, IBM, Microsoft SQL Server, or any other vendor. Think of the different vendors and implementations (RDBMSs) as makes and models of different cars. The buttons and switches and cup holders might be in a slightly different place, but the fundamental mechanics, the brake and the gas pedal, will be in the same place and will operate as expected. The goal of SQL is to ask good questions. If you set your sights on this goal, the rest will fall into place. If you would like some further information on the subject of SQL implementations, there is a website called https://db-engines.com/en/ranking that features a helpful tool to see which database implementations are currently the most utilized.

Switching Careers

"If the bulk of my professional experience comes from a field far removed from SQL or programming, how do I convince my employer to give me a chance as a data analyst?" This is a concern I hear from many of my students that come from a completely different professional background and are just starting with data analysis. Data is far less removed from your previous profession than you think! Let's say you were a bus driver. At first you may think a profession like this is far removed from that of a data analyst, but what we've seen is that the language of data has permeated everything. On every bus route, you have seen which stops have more people, which routes are the most efficient, etc. In any profession, the data is all around you. Even if your current line of work doesn't have a database, you could start collecting information on every bus ride and present that information to your employer. Even if you come from a nontechnical field, you can use the skills you learned in this book to capture data from any walk of life and turn it into information. If a database doesn't exist, you can create one!

Selling Your New Skills to Your Company

I sometimes get questions from my students about how to convince their company to give them a chance with database access, particularly if they joined the company with a completely different job description. "I have explained that my queries will not change the database in any way, yet they are still reluctant to give me even read access. How do I change their minds?" As for the practical method of how to get the stakeholders of your business venture to buy into your new profession, this is usually not a problem, since databases are designed to be queried and accessed without changing the data. However, a company may choose to restrict database access to only a few key individuals. There are a variety of reasons database restrictions might occur, but in these cases, it is important to sell yourself and emphasize the value of turning data into information, as we have done in this book. Explain how what you are doing is going to save the company money in the long run. In most scenarios, databases have three environments: development, testing, and production. You can request access to the development environment or, if the database is quite small, ask for a copy. But there is a greater point here. Don't let a small roadblock deter you from your goal; data is everywhere. As Bob Marley said, "When one door is closed, don't you know another is open?"

You might even be able to find a similar database in the same field as that of your company. There are public repositories of data (such as data.gov for the United States) that will help you practice your skills.

Beyond SQL: Data Visualization Software

There is much more developing in the world of data science other than just SQL. For the student eager to expand their skills beyond writing queries in a text-based SQL browser, data visualization is a good pathway. Presenting information is a pain point for many people. As you have seen from our use of DB Browser and the SQLite implementation, the backbone of SQL still very much exists in the highly functional but visually unappealing world of script-like programming languages.

Data visualization software (also known as business intelligence software) is a hot field that is growing right now. Visualization can give new life to plain SQL statements. We have seen in this book that things like views can help you save frequently used queries and present information in a consistent and more organized way. Visualization software takes views one step further and gives you the ability to add bar charts, pivot tables, and other ways of displaying data. Visualization software also allows data to be displayed in real time so your fields and derivative visuals, such as charts or graphs, automatically update as the data changes. This beats the old way of copying data to a spreadsheet program like Excel and developing visuals from there. Figure 128 shows the names of a few popular data visualization software packages. This list is not exhaustive, but it will give you a good place to start.

fig. 128

Interview Advice

I see a lot of online articles offering lists of technical things you "must know" before interviewing for any SQL-related job. Sometimes those "top ten technical skills you must know" are about as helpful as the "top ten animals that can kill you" lists found on any clickbait website. I do not consider myself someone who excels at highly technical interviews, such as the ones that ask you to memorize syntax and apply it to a very specific scenario. I consider myself much better at seeing the big picture, taking a technical challenge or business question presented and walking the interviewer through the steps required to get to the desired result. If the bar of acceptance or rejection to a career opportunity relies on memorization or a dramatic display of technical aptitude, this may be a red flag about how the company views its tech solutions. It is much better if the organization is more interested in the way that I solve problems in my own unique creative style than if I can commit syntax to memory. Some interviewers may focus on a specific tool, such as the syntax of a view, or may ask you to solve a problem using a certain type of SQL statement. This interviewing technique is shortsighted, in my opinion, focusing on muscle memory. It is much more valuable to see how creative a potential employee's thought process is when applying a view or other SQL solution toward solving the problem.

SQL Certifications

There are many different certification programs available for SQL and database administration. Examples of the most common certifications are the Microsoft Certified Solutions Associate (MCSA) and the Microsoft Certified Solutions Expert (MCSE). However, the Microsoft pathways are not the only options. There are other database platforms such as Oracle and IBM, which are also major players in the database sphere that offer certifications. Are certifications really necessary? Certification is not the only route to take in your SQL career. I firmly believe that you can get as much, if not more, value with a more practical approach. To me, the ability to actually use the language is more important than the certification. If your company uses IBM, go ahead and get the certification. But if you are not sure, then just focus on practicing solving real-world questions with whatever implementation you see yourself using.

Final Thoughts and Parting Words

It is my sincere hope that you have enjoyed this book and that I have instilled in you some of the passion I have for this subject. If you would like to learn more about what we do at my data visualization company, and the training courses I offer, you can find me at http://datadecided.com and https://sqltrainingwheels.com. It has been my pleasure to accompany you on this journey so far.

REMEMBER TO DOWNLOAD
YOUR FREE DIGITAL ASSETS!

 Free Audiobook Version of This Book*

 Sample Database (required for examples)

 SQL Software Download Links & Instructions

 SQL Statement Reference Guide

 Video Tutorial

DOWNLOAD DIGITAL ASSETS NOW:

www.clydebankmedia.com/sql-assets

Appendix I
Data Analysis Checkpoint Questions and Solutions

Chapter 3 Data Analysis Checkpoint

Using the Database Structure tab and the Browse Data tab, try to answer the following questions:

Question 1: How many tables are in our database?

Solution: Looking at the Database Structure tab in DB Browser, the number of tables is calculated for us and presented in parentheses ( ). There are thirteen tables in this database.

fig. 129

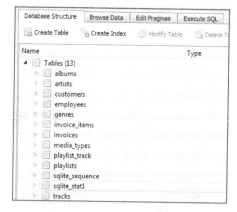

Question 2: How many fields does the table named *tracks* have?

Solution: For any of the tables listed, we can click on the small right-facing triangle to see the columns for that table.

fig. 130

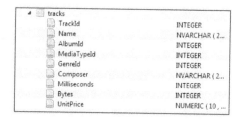

In this example, we observe that the table called *tracks* has nine columns.

Question 3: What are some of the data types in this table?

Solution: If we look at the image from the previous question, we can see that the TrackId column accepts data of the type INTEGER and the Name column accepts data of the type NVARCHAR. The rest of the columns are also INTEGER and NVARCHAR except for UnitPrice, which is a NUMERIC data type.

Question 4: What does the actual data look like in the table?

Solution: Now we can swap to the Browse Data tab and actually look at the table. We need to make sure to select the *tracks* table in the drop-down menu. Looking at the data in the table shows us why an INTEGER data type is used for columns like TrackId and AlbumId, while a character data type makes more sense for the Name and Composer columns. Finally, for UnitPrice, we needed something with decimals, so the integer data type wouldn't have been sufficient for this column.

IMAGE

fig. 131

Table:	tracks								
	TrackId	Name	AlbumId	MediaTypeId	GenreId	Composer	Milliseconds	Bytes	UnitPrice
	Filter	Filter	Filter	Filter	Filter	Filter	Filter	Filter	Filter
1	1	For Those Ab...	1	1	1	Angus Young,...	343719	11170334	0.99
2	2	Balls to the Wall	2	2	1		342562	5510424	0.99
3	3	Fast As a Shark	3	2	1	F. Baltes, S. K...	230619	3990994	0.99
4	4	Restless and ...	3	2	1	F. Baltes, R.A....	252051	4331779	0.99
5	5	Princess of th...	3	2	1	Deaffy & R.A. ...	375418	6290521	0.99

Database Structure Browse Data Edit Pragmas Execute SQL

Chapter 4 Data Analysis Checkpoint

Question 1: How many customers' last names begin with *B*?

Solution: In order to answer this question, we can first write a query to display the specific information we are looking for. In this case, we are interested in last names. Last names are contained in the *customers* table under the field name LastName.

If we simply want a query to display all the last names, we can do this:

```
SELECT
    LastName
FROM
    customers
```

That will give us a field of all the last names, but they aren't in any particular order. To alphabetize them we can use the ORDER BY statement. Note that we don't have to specify A-Z because ascending order is returned by default. If we were looking for names starting with Z, we might have included the DESC statement.

```
SELECT
    LastName
FROM
    customers
ORDER BY
LastName ASC
```

GRAPHIC

fig. 132

	LastName
1	Almeida
2	Barnett
3	Bernard
4	Brooks
5	Brown
6	Chase
7	Cunningham
8	Dubois
9	Fernandes
10	Francis
...	

Now our results are alphabetized and we can easily see that four of the entries start with *B*. Note that we are still using observation to determine how many entries start with *B*. Other ways to do this will be explored further on.

Question 2: When sorted in descending order, which company appears at the top, in the *customers* table?

Solution: This time we are looking for the Company field instead of the LastName field. As mentioned in the last question, all we have to do is change the last part of our query to specify descending order.

```
SELECT
    Company
FROM
    customers
ORDER BY
    Company DESC
```

Doing this yields the following result:

fig. 133

	Company
1	Woodstock Discos
2	Telus
3	Rogers Canada
4	Riotur
5	Microsoft Corporation
6	JetBrains s.r.o.
7	Google Inc.
8	Embraer - Empresa Brasileira de Aeronáutica S.A.
9	Banco do Brasil S.A.
10	Apple Inc.
...	

We can observe that Woodstock Discos is the first company listed in descending order.

Question 3: How many customers do not have a postal code listed?

Solution: We could answer this question by scrolling through the data on Browse Data, but there is a better way. Using a SELECT statement, we can list all the data in ascending order as we have done previously. But this time, we want to list more than just one column, so we can see what customer names have no postal code data. So we can choose FirstName, LastName, and PostalCode, then order the results by PostalCode.

```
SELECT
    FirstName,
    LastName,
    PostalCode
FROM
    customers
ORDER BY
    PostalCode
```

This shows us four entries that do not have postal data, as designated by the null value in the PostalCode column (Figure 134).

	FirstName	LastName	PostalCode
1	João	Fernandes	NULL
2	Madalena	Sampaio	NULL
3	Hugh	O'Reilly	NULL
4	Luís	Rojas	NULL
5	Stanisław	Wójcik	00-358
6	Lucas	Mancini	00192
7	Terhi	Hämäläinen	00530
8	Eduardo	Martins	01007-010
9	Alexandre	Rocha	01310-200
10	Bjørn	Hansen	0171
...			

GRAPHIC

fig. 134

NOTE

If we were to list these in descending order, we would have to scroll to the bottom to see the null values.

Chapter 5 Data Analysis Checkpoint

Question 1: Create a query for th*e invoices* table that includes a CASE statement that labels all sales from billing country USA as "Domestic Sales" and all other sales as "Foreign Sales." Label your new field as SalesType after your END AS statement.

Solution: To display this information, we combine what we learned about filtering records by text with our CASE statement. Since we are categorizing our CASE statement by billing country, we will have to include that field in our SELECT statement.

```
SELECT
    InvoiceDate,
    BillingAddress,
    BillingCity,
    BillingCountry,
    Total,
    CASE
    WHEN BillingCountry = 'USA' THEN 'Domestic Sales'
    ELSE 'Foreign Sales'
    END AS SalesType
FROM
    invoices
```

	InvoiceDate	BillingAddress	BillingCity	BillingCountry	Total	PurchaseType
1	1/1/2009 0:00	Theodor-Heuss-Straße 34	Stuttgart	Germany	1.98	Foreign Sales
2	1/2/2009 0:00	Ullevålsveien 14	Oslo	Norway	3.96	Foreign Sales
3	1/3/2009 0:00	Grétrystraat 63	Brussels	Belgium	5.94	Foreign Sales
4	1/6/2009 0:00	8210 111 ST NW	Edmonton	Canada	8.91	Foreign Sales
5	1/11/2009 0:00	69 Salem Street	Boston	USA	13.86	Domestic Sales
6	1/19/2009 0:00	Berger Straße 10	Frankfurt	Germany	0.99	Foreign Sales
7	2/1/2009 0:00	Barbarossastraße 19	Berlin	Germany	1.98	Foreign Sales
8	2/1/2009 0:00	8, Rue Hanovre	Paris	France	1.98	Foreign Sales
9	2/2/2009 0:00	9, Place Louis Barthou	Bordeaux	France	3.96	Foreign Sales
10	2/3/2009 0:00	3 Chatham Street	Dublin	Ireland	5.94	Foreign Sales
...						

fig. 135

Question 2: Order this data by the new field `SalesType`.

Solution: To show all domestic sales in one group and all foreign sales in another group, we simply add an ORDER BY (using our new field) to our existing query:

```
SELECT
    InvoiceDate,
    BillingAddress,
    BillingCity,
    BillingCountry,
    Total,
    CASE
    WHEN BillingCountry = 'USA' THEN 'Domestic Sales'
    ELSE 'Foreign Sales'
    END AS SalesType
FROM
    invoices
ORDER BY
    SalesType
```

Figure 136 shows the results for this query displaying "Domestic Sales" first, if you run this query and scroll down, you will see all countries other than USA labled as "Foreign Sales.".

fig. 136

	InvoiceDate	BillingAddress	BillingCity	BillingCountry	Total	SalesType
1	1/11/2009 0:00	69 Salem Street	Boston	USA	13.86	Domestic Sales
2	2/19/2009 0:00	1600 Amphitheatre Parkway	Mountain View	USA	0.99	Domestic Sales
3	3/4/2009 0:00	1 Microsoft Way	Redmond	USA	1.98	Domestic Sales
4	3/4/2009 0:00	1 Infinite Loop	Cupertino	USA	1.98	Domestic Sales
5	3/5/2009 0:00	801 W 4th Street	Reno	USA	3.96	Domestic Sales
6	3/6/2009 0:00	319 N. Frances Street	Madison	USA	5.94	Domestic Sales
7	4/14/2009 0:00	1 Infinite Loop	Cupertino	USA	13.86	Domestic Sales
8	6/6/2009 0:00	1 Microsoft Way	Redmond	USA	3.96	Domestic Sales
9	6/7/2009 0:00	801 W 4th Street	Reno	USA	5.94	Domestic Sales
10	6/10/2009 0:00	1033 N Park Ave	Tucson	USA	8.91	Domestic Sales
...						

Question 3: How many invoices from Domestic Sales were over $15?

Solution: We can use the same query again, but this time add a WHERE clause and AND to include both the numeric and text parameters.

```
SELECT
    InvoiceDate,
    BillingAddress,
    BillingCity,
    BillingCountry,
    Total,
    CASE
    WHEN BillingCountry = 'USA' THEN 'Domestic Sales'
    ELSE 'ForeignSales'
    END AS SalesType
FROM
    invoices
Where
    SalesType = "Domestic Sales" AND Total > 15
```

fig. 137

	InvoiceDate	BillingAddress	BillingCity	BillingCountry	Total	SalesType
1	3/21/2010 0:00	162 E Superior Street	Chicago	USA	15.86	Domestic Sales
2	5/29/2011 0:00	319 N. Frances Street	Madison	USA	18.86	Domestic Sales
3	8/5/2012 0:00	2211 W Berry Street	Fort Worth	USA	23.86	Domestic Sales

Chapter 6 Data Analysis Checkpoint

Question 1: Using DB Browser and the Browse Data tab or the entity relationship diagram on page 95, view the *tracks* table. Identify which fields in that table are foreign keys in another table. Based on the foreign keys you have identified, which tables are related to the *tracks* table?

Solution: Looking at the *tracks* table, we see three fields with integer values that appear to be foreign keys.

fig. 138

	TrackId	Name	AlbumId	MediaTypeId	GenreId	Composer	Milliseconds	Bytes	UnitPrice
	Filter	Filter	Filter	Filter	Filter	Filter	Filter	Filter	Filter
1	1	For Those Ab...	1	1	1	Angus Young,...	343719	11170334	0.99
2	2	Balls to the Wall	2	2	1		342562	5510424	0.99
3	3	Fast As a Shark	3	2	1	F. Baltes, S. K...	230619	3990994	0.99
4	4	Restless and ...	3	2	1	F. Baltes, R.A...	252051	4331779	0.99
5	5	Princess of th...	3	2	1	Deaffy & R.A. ...	375418	6290521	0.99
6	6	Put The Finge...	1	1	1	Angus Young,...	205662	6713451	0.99
7	7	Let's Get It Up	1	1	1	Angus Young,...	233926	7636561	0.99
8	8	Inject The Ve...	1	1	1	Angus Young,...	210834	6852860	0.99
9	9	Snowballed	1	1	1	Angus Young,...	203102	6599424	0.99
10	10	Evil Walks	1	1	1	Angus Young,...	263497	8611245	0.99

The fields `AlbumId`, `MediaTypeId`, and `GenreId` correspond to the *albums*, *media_types*, and *genres* tables, respectively.

Question 2: Create an inner join between the *albums* and *tracks* tables to display corresponding artist names, album titles, and track names in a single result set.

Solution:

```
SELECT
    t.composer AS "Artist Name",
    a.title AS "Album Title",
    t.Name AS "Track Name"
FROM
    albums a
INNER JOIN
    tracks t
ON
    a.AlbumId = t.AlbumId
```

Question 3: Using the *genres* table identified in question 1, create a third inner join to join to this table and include the `Name` field from that table in your result set.

Solution:

```sql
SELECT
    g.name AS Genre,
    t.composer AS "Artist Name",
    a.title AS "Album Title",
    t.Name AS "Track Name"
FROM
    albums a
INNER JOIN
    tracks t
ON
    a.AlbumId = t.AlbumId
INNER JOIN
    genres g
ON
    g.GenreId = t.GenreId
```

Chapter 7 Data Analysis Checkpoint

Question 1: Create a single-line mailing list for all US customers, including capitalized full names and full addresses with five-digit zip codes, in the following format:

FRANK HARRIS 1600 Amphitheatre Parkway, Mountain View, CA 94043

Solution: The format above is calling for the first and last names to be in all caps, so we will need the UPPER() function for those two fields. We use the double pipes to concatenate the rest of the fields, adding spaces and commas where needed.

```sql
SELECT
    UPPER(FirstName) || ' ' || UPPER(LastName) || ' '
    || Address || ', ' || City || ', ' || State || ' '
    || SUBSTR(PostalCode,1,5) AS [MailingAddress]
FROM
    customers
WHERE
    Country = 'USA'
```

	MailingAddress
1	FRANK HARRIS 1600 Amphitheatre Parkway, Mountain View, CA 94043
2	JACK SMITH 1 Microsoft Way, Redmond, WA 98052
3	MICHELLE BROOKS 627 Broadway, New York, NY 10012
4	TIM GOYER 1 Infinite Loop, Cupertino, CA 95014
5	DAN MILLER 541 Del Medio Avenue, Mountain View, CA 94040
1	KATHY CHASE 801 W 4th Street, Reno, NV 89503
2	HEATHER LEACOCK 120 S Orange Ave, Orlando, FL 32801
3	JOHN GORDON 69 Salem Street, Boston, MA 2113
4	FRANK RALSTON 162 E Superior Street, Chicago, IL 60611
5	VICTOR STEVENS 319 N. Frances Street, Madison, WI 53703
...	

fig. 139

Question 2: What are the average annual sales generated by customers from the USA from all years of data available?

Solution: If we are just looking for an aggregate function for one country, we can simply select billing country and the average of the total using the WHERE clause to limit our results to the USA.

```
SELECT
    BillingCountry,
    AVG(Total)
FROM
    invoices
WHERE
    BillingCountry = 'USA'
```

	BillingCountry	AVG(Total)
1	USA	5.7479121

fig. 140

We can use the ROUND() function outside of the AVG() function to reduce the number of decimal places returned.

Question 3: What are the company's all-time total sales?

Solution: Since this question is asking us for the sum total of invoices, our SELECT statement is fairly simple.

```
SELECT
    SUM(Total)
FROM
    invoices
```

fig. 141

	SUM(Total)
1	2328.6

Question 4: Who are the top ten best customers from a revenue standpoint? *Hint:* you will need to use a join (chapter 6) to answer this question.

Solution: We have already found the total revenue. Now we are looking for the top ten customers responsible for the highest revenue. Since we are looking for data from one table that corresponds to data from another table in a one-to-one relationship, we use an inner join.

```
SELECT
    SUM(Total)AS [Revenue Total],
    c.FirstName,
    c.LastName
FROM
    invoices i
INNER JOIN
    customers c
ON
    i.CustomerId = c.CustomerId
GROUP BY c.CustomerId
ORDER BY SUM(Total) DESC
```

Chapter 8 Data Analysis Checkpoint

Question 1: How many invoices exceed the average invoice amount generated in 2010?

Solution: To answer this question we need to accomplish two tasks. First we need to find the average invoice amount generated in 2010. Second, we need to compare that value with every invoice in our table to see how many exceeded the average 2010 invoice value.

First let's write our subquery:

```
select
    avg(total)
from
    invoices
where
    InvoiceDate between '2010-01-01' and '2010-12-31'
```

Running this query gives us an average of $5.80; now we need to write the outer query to select invoices that are greater than the 2010 average.

```
SELECT
    InvoiceDate,
    Total
FROM
    invoices
WHERE
Total >

(select
    avg(total)
from
    invoices
where
    InvoiceDate between '2010-01-01' and '2010-12-31')
ORDER BY
    Total DESC
```

GRAPHIC

fig. 142

	InvoiceDate	Total
1	11/13/2013 0:00	25.86
2	8/5/2012 0:00	23.86
3	2/18/2010 0:00	21.86
4	4/28/2011 0:00	21.86
5	1/18/2010 0:00	18.86
6	5/29/2011 0:00	18.86
7	1/13/2010 0:00	17.91
8	9/5/2012 0:00	16.86
9	10/6/2012 0:00	16.86
10	3/21/2010 0:00	15.86
...		

Our Results Pane tells us that 179 results were returned.

NOTE

> If we only wanted the actual number of invoices returned, we could modify our `Total` field in our outer query to say `COUNT(Total)`.

Question 2: Who are the customers responsible for these invoices?

Solution: This problem requires joins again, to connect customer data from the *customers* table to the *invoices* table. The question itself implies a one-to-one relationship between the *customers* table and the *invoices* table. We have already selected the invoices we are interested in, so now we need to find the customers attached to those invoices. This is exactly what an inner join does. This solution is very similar to the solution to Question 1. All we have added is the inner join section so we have access to customer names as well.

```
SELECT
    i.InvoiceDate,
    i.Total,
    c.FirstName,
    c.LastName
FROM
    invoices i
INNER JOIN
    customers c
ON
    i.CustomerId = c.CustomerId
WHERE
Total >

(select
    avg(total)
from
    invoices
where
    InvoiceDate between '2010-01-01' and '2010-12-31')
ORDER BY
    Total DESC
```

Question 3: How many of these customers are from the USA?

Solution: We can modify the solution to Question 2 above to include an AND statement at the end of the WHERE clause of the outer query.

```
SELECT
    InvoiceDate,
    Total,
    BillingCountry
FROM
    invoices
WHERE
Total >

(select
    avg(total)
from
    invoices
where
    InvoiceDate between '2010-01-01' and '2010-12-31')
AND BillingCountry = 'USA'
ORDER BY
    Total DESC
```

GRAPHIC

fig. 143

	InvoiceDate	Total	BillingCountry
1	11/13/2013 0:00	25.86	USA
2	8/5/2012 0:00	23.86	USA
3	2/18/2010 0:00	21.86	USA
4	4/28/2011 0:00	21.86	USA
5	1/18/2010 0:00	18.86	USA
6	5/29/2011 0:00	18.86	USA
7	1/13/2010 0:00	17.91	USA
8	9/5/2012 0:00	16.86	USA
9	10/6/2012 0:00	16.86	USA
10	3/21/2010 0:00	15.86	USA
...			

Our Results Pane shows us that the query returned forty records.

We could use a SUM() function around the total if we wanted this query to return the exact number of results.

Chapter 9 Data Analysis Checkpoint

In this checkpoint we asked you to turn the following query, which compares average invoice per city against the global average, into a series of views:

```
SELECT
    BillingCity,
    AVG(Total) AS [City Average],
    (select
            avg(total)
    from
            invoices) AS [Global Average]
FROM
    invoices
GROUP BY
    BillingCity
ORDER BY
    BillingCity
```

Question 1: Take the inner query (by itself) from this SELECT statement and create a view from it. Save the view as V_GlobalAverage.

If you have been following along with the in-chapter examples, you might have already saved an average function as a view. For this exercise, make sure this new view has a new name.

Solution: We take the inner query by itself and add the view syntax on the first line.

```
CREATE VIEW V_GlobalAverage AS
select
    avg(total)
from
    invoices AS [Global Average]
```

Question 2: Remove the subquery from the code above entirely and substitute it with your newly created view V_GlobalAverage.

Solution: When we use a view in the SELECT clause, we use the asterisk symbol.

```
SELECT
    BillingCity,
    AVG(Total) AS [City Average],
(select
    *
from
V_GlobalAverage) AS [Global Average]
FROM
    invoices
GROUP BY
    BillingCity
ORDER BY
    BillingCity
```

Question 3: Save this new query as a view called V_CityAvgVsGlobalAvg.

Solution: We copy our code from question 2 and add the CREATE VIEW statement at the very top.

```
CREATE VIEW V_CityAvgVsGlobalAvg AS
SELECT
    BillingCity,
    AVG(Total) AS [City Average],
(select
    *
from
V_GlobalAverage) AS [Global Average]
FROM
    invoices
GROUP BY
    BillingCity
ORDER BY
    BillingCity
```

Question 4: Delete the view V_GlobalAverage. What happens to V_CityAvgVsGlobalAvg?

Solution: We use DROP VIEW to delete our view. Alternatively, we can right-click on the view from our Database Structure tab in DB Browser and delete the view that way.

```
DROP VIEW V_GlobalAverage
```

Now to see how this impacts our previous statements, we need to write a SELECT statement to select our virtual table.

```
V_CityAvgVsGlobalAvg
SELECT
    *
FROM
    V_CityAvgVsGlobalAvg
```

You should get the following error message:

```
no such table: main.V_GlobalAverage:
```

Chapter 10 Data Analysis Checkpoint

Question 1: Add a new customer to the database.

Solution: We first need to add our new customer to the *customers* table. A customer can exist alone without being referenced on any other table (if they didn't make a purchase yet). To start, insert a record into the *customers* table.

```
INSERT INTO
customers
VALUES ('60', 'New', 'Customer', '', '123 Day Street',
'New York', 'NY', 'USA', '11201', '(347) 525-8688', '',
'nc@gmail.com', '1');
```

We left some of the fields as null by including two single quotes next to each other. We can check our work by running a SELECT statement that looks for the name of the customer we just added.

```
SELECT
*
FROM
customers
WHERE
FirstName = 'New'
```

NOTE

If you used a different name for your new customer, modify that value in the query accordingly.

GRAPHIC

	CustomerId	FirstName	LastName	Company	Address	City	State	Country	PostalCode	Phone	Fax	Email	SupportId
1	60	New	Customer		123 Day Street	New York	NY	USA	11201	(347)525-8688		nc@gmail.com	1

fig. 144

Question 2: Create an invoice record for this customer.

Solution: In order to create an invoice entry for our new customer, we must pay special attention to the fields in the *invoices* table that correspond to our *customers* table. For example, our invoices use the same address that appears in the *customers* table.

```
INSERT INTO
invoices
VALUES ('413', '60', '2019-10-04 00:00:00', '123 Day
Street', 'New York', 'NY', 'USA', '10201', '50.00')
```

Question 3: Remove this customer from the database.

Solution: As we mentioned in chapter 10, it is a best practice to view the data we are going to delete so that we can see what we will be deleting. In this case, the data we are deleting stretches across two tables, so we write an INNER JOIN statement to view all the data we have included.

```
SELECT
    c.FirstName,
    c.LastName,
    i.Total,
    i.InvoiceId
FROM
    invoices i
```

```
INNER JOIN
    customers c
ON      i.CustomerId = c.CustomerId
WHERE c.CustomerId = 60
```

Now that we have confirmed the data, we can compose the DELETE statement.

```
DELETE FROM
    invoices
WHERE CustomerId = 60

DELETE FROM
    customers
WHERE CustomerId = 60
```

Appendix II

List of SQL Keywords by Chapter

Chapter 4 Keywords

```
SELECT, AS, FROM, ORDER BY, ASC, DESC, LIMIT
```

```
/*
This is a block comment. Block comments start with a forward slash followed
by the asterisk, then end with an asterisk and another forward slash. Block
comments should usually follow this format:

CREATED BY: <your name>
CREATED ON: <date>
DESCRIPTION: <Brief description of what your query does>
*/



-- This is an example of using a single-line comment:

SELECT -- Specifies what data or fields to retrieve from the database
    FirstName AS 'First Name', - These are field names
    LastName AS [Last Name], - The AS keyword renames the field
    Company AS Co - One-word aliases do not need single quotes or parentheses

FROM -- Specifies the table containing the desired data
    customers - Refers to the customers table

ORDER BY -- Specifies the output order; ascending (A-Z) is the default
    FirstName DESC - Typing DESC specifies descending (Z-A) order

LIMIT -- Limits results to a specific number
    10; - The semicolon is optional here
```

Chapter 5 Keywords

```
WHERE, CASE, WHEN, THEN, ELSE, END AS, DATE()
```

Operators in SQL are used within SQL clauses.

TYPES OF OPERATORS

fig. 145

COMPARISON	LOGICAL	ARITHMETIC
= Equal To	BETWEEN	+ Add
> Greater Than	IN	- Subtract
< Less Than	LIKE	/ Divide
>= Greater Than or Equal To	AND	* Multiply
<= Less Than or Equal To	OR	% Modulo
<> Not Equal To		

```
SELECT
    InvoiceDate,
    BillingAddress,
    BillingCity,
    Total
FROM
    invoices
WHERE
Total = 1.98 -- Only returns records where the field Total is equal to 1.98
ORDER BY
    InvoiceDate

CASE - This statement allows you to filter records by user-specified condi...
    WHEN -- Used with a case statement to specify a condition
    THEN -- Used with a case statement after WHEN to create a label for all...
    ELSE -- Used to specify every condition not covered by the WHEN/THEN...
    END AS -- Creates a new field for the labels created by the ELSE state...

SELECT
    InvoiceDate,
    BillingAddress,
    BillingCity,
    Total,
CASE -- Creates four conditions to display different price ranges for the...
    WHEN TOTAL < 2.00 THEN 'Baseline Purchase' - Condition 1
    WHEN TOTAL BETWEEN 2.00 AND 6.99 THEN 'Low Purchase'
    WHEN TOTAL BETWEEN 7.00 AND 15.00 THEN 'Target Purchase'
ELSE 'Top Performers' -- The ELSE keyword handles all other conditions not...
    END AS PurchaseType
FROM
    invoices
ORDER BY
    BillingCity
```

The single-line comments are abbreviated in the previous example for the sake of print. Single-line comments must always be on one line in the SQL browser or they will be mistaken for code and will result in errors.

fig. 146

	InvoiceDate	BillingAddress	BillingCity	Total	PurchaseType
1	2009-05-10 00:00:00	Lijnbaansgracht 120bg	Amsterdam	8.91	Target Purchase
2	2010-12-15 00:00:00	Lijnbaansgracht 120bg	Amsterdam	1.98	Baseline Purchase
3	2011-03-19 00:00:00	Lijnbaansgracht 120bg	Amsterdam	3.96	Low Purchase
...	...	...	...	...	...
71	2010-03-21 00:00:00	162 E Superior Street	Chicago	15.86	Top Performers

DATE() is the first function introduced in the book. It is introduced early so it can be used with the other keywords in chapter 5. More functions are introduced in chapter 7.

```
/*
The DATE() function removes any timecode information
from data stored as DATETIME.
*/
SELECT
    InvoiceDate,
    DATE(InvoiceDate) AS [Results of DATE Function]
FROM
    invoices
ORDER BY
    InvoiceDate
```

fig. 147

	InvoiceDate	Results of DATE Function
1	2009-01-01 00:00:00	2009-01-01
2	2009-01-02 00:00:00	2009-01-02
3	2009-01-03 00:00:00	2009-01-03
4	2009-01-06 00:00:00	2009-01-06
5	2009-01-11 00:00:00	2009-01-11
...		

Chapter 6 Keywords

INNER JOIN, ON, LEFT OUTER JOIN, RIGHT OUTER JOIN, IS, NOT

NOTE

The RIGHT JOIN is not supported in SQLite but is supported in other RDBMS implementations.

INNER JOIN

```
SELECT
    i.InvoiceId, -- Alias notation specifies what table the field is from
    c.CustomerId,
    c.Name,
    c.Address,
    i.InvoiceDate,
    i.BillingAddress,
    i.Total
FROM
    invoices AS i
INNER JOIN
    customers AS c
ON i.CustomerId = c.CustomerId
```

LEFT OUTER JOIN

```
SELECT
    i.InvoiceId,
    c.CustomerId,
    c.Name,
    c.Address,
    i.InvoiceDate,
    i.BillingAddress,
    i.Total
FROM
    invoices AS i
LEFT OUTER JOIN
    customers AS c
ON
    i.CustomerId = c.CustomerId
```

RIGHT OUTER JOIN (Not Supported in SQLite)

```
SELECT
    i.InvoiceId,
    c.CustomerId,
    c.Name,
    c.Address,
    i.InvoiceDate,
    i.BillingAddress,
    i.Total
FROM
    invoices AS i
RIGHT OUTER JOIN -- Switch position of tables listed in query to create L...
    customers AS c
ON i.CustomerId = c.CustomerId


SELECT
    ar.ArtistId AS [ArtistId From Artists Table],
    al.ArtistId AS [ArtistId From Albums Table],
    ar.Name AS [Artist Name],
    al.Title AS [Album]
FROM
    artists AS ar
LEFT OUTER JOIN
    albums AS al
ON
    ar.ArtistId = al.ArtistId
WHERE
    al.ArtistId IS NULL - Can also use IS NOT
```

Chapter 7 Keywords

```
GROUP BY, HAVING
```

TYPES OF FUNCTIONS

fig. 148

STRING	DATE	AGGREGATE
INSTR()	DATE()	AVG()
LENGTH()	DATETIME()	COUNT()
LOWER()	JULIANDAY()	MAX()
LTRIM()	STRFTIME()	MIN()
REPLACE()	TIME()	SUM()
RTRIM()	'NOW'	
SUBSTR()		
TRIM()		
UPPER()		

⟵——— || (double pipes concatenation)

Miscellaneous Functions: Round()

Chapter 8 Keywords

DISTINCT

The basic subquery:

IMAGE

fig. 149

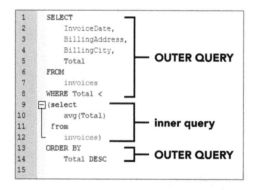

```
1   SELECT
2       InvoiceDate,
3       BillingAddress,
4       BillingCity,               OUTER QUERY
5       Total
6   FROM
7       invoices
8   WHERE Total <
9   ⊟(select
10      avg(Total)                 inner query
11  from
12      invoices)
13  ORDER BY
14      Total DESC                 OUTER QUERY
15
```

GRAPHIC

fig. 150

	TrackId
1	1
2	2
3	3
4	4
5	5
6	6
7	8
8	9
9	10
10	12
...	1984 rows returned in 11ms

The DISTINCT clause:

```
SELECT
    DISTINCT TrackId
FROM
    invoice_items
ORDER BY
    TrackId
```

Chapter 9 Keywords

```
CREATE VIEW, DROP VIEW
```

```
CREATE VIEW V_ViewName AS [Alias Name]

DROP VIEW V_ViewName
```

Chapter 10 Keywords

```
INSERT INTO, UPDATE, SET, DELETE
```

 Data manipulation language (DML) can permanently alter a database. It is best to practice these commands in a sandbox space such as the sample database provided. Using DML on a live database with active customer data can have permanent deleterious effects.

```
INSERT INTO
artists (Name)
VALUES ('Bob Marley')


UPDATE
employees
SET PostalCode = '11202'
WHERE
   EmployeeId = 9


DELETE FROM
   employees
WHERE
   EmployeeId = 9
```

WHAT DID YOU THINK?

Thank you for choosing a bestselling ClydeBank Media *QuickStart Guide*™.

This book represents the hard work and dedication of not only the author but numerous members of our expert team. We hope this book presented a simplified and valuable look at the subject matter at hand. Our goal is to be your partner on this learning path and to provide relevant and practical information that can be put to use in your life right away.

So, how did we do?

Our independent publishing company relies on honest and objective feedback from readers like you. Your feedback helps us improve our books to better serve our customers and helps them to stand out on online retailers so new readers who are searching for simplified and beginner-friendly learning material can discover our library of titles more easily.

We would greatly appreciate it if you could take a few seconds to let us know what you thought of this book by visiting the URL below. All feedback is welcome, both positive and critical. What did you like? What did you learn? What surprised you, or what did you put into action right away? Share your thoughts with us and with others who have yet to discover us!

To leave your feedback please visit: www.clydebankmedia.com/sql-review

If you need assistance with an order, have questions or comments, or want to reach out to our team directly, please send us an email at support@clydebankmedia.com.

About the Author

WALTER SHIELDS

Walter Shields has worked with SQL and databases for over eighteen years, helping organizations such as Target Corporation, NYC Transit Authority, and NYC Administration for Children's Services successfully leverage and understand their data using SQL.

While Walter's self-described path through the emerging industry of data science in the late 1990s was anything but straightforward, he firmly believed that SQL did not have to be so daunting for everyone else. Walter's desire to simplify the learning process eventually led him to start teaching students in a coffee shop in Tribeca, New York, equipped with nothing but a laptop full of SQL learning materials. Since then, his mentorship has turned into its own business: SQL Training Wheels. When not teaching students, Walter can be found working on his latest project, Datadecided, a Tableau-based data visualization company that helps medium and large businesses leverage their data with actionable data visualizations. You can reach Walter at www.sqltrainingwheels.com and learn more about Tableau and data visualization at www.Datadecided.com.

About ClydeBank Media

We create simplified educational tools that allow our customers to successfully learn new skills in order to navigate this constantly changing world.

The success of ClydeBank Media's value-driven approach starts with beginner-friendly high-quality information. We work with subject matter experts who are leaders in their fields. These experts are supported by our team of professional researchers, writers, and educators.

Our team at ClydeBank Media works with these industry leaders to break down their wealth of knowledge, their wisdom, and their years of experience into small and concise building blocks. We piece together these building blocks to create a clearly defined learning path that a beginner can follow for successful mastery.

At ClydeBank Media, we see a new world of possibility. Simplified learning doesn't have to be bound by four walls; instead, it's driven by you.

Glossary

Aggregate Function
A function designed to produce a single result based on the contents of an entire field. Aggregate functions can return a sum, a minimum, a maximum, a count, or other mathematical functions.

Alias
A substitute name for a database column defined by the user in an AS statement. An alias is used for clarity or presentation when displaying a query.

Argument
A parameter of a function, usually encased in parentheses () and separated by a comma.

Arithmetic Operator
An SQL keyword used to perform basic arithmetic operations (add, subtract, multiply, divide, modulo) usually within a WHERE clause.

Attribute
Another representation of a field.

Boolean
A data type expressed as either true or false.

Clause
A subsection of an SQL statement that starts with a reserved keyword and may include additional parameters and operators.

Coding Convention
A set of guidelines, standards, and best practices used in most programming languages to ensure that code is readable by other company stakeholders.

Column
Another representation of a field.

Comparison Operator
An SQL keyword used to compare values, usually used within a WHERE clause. Examples include "=" (equal to), ">" (greater than), "<" (less than), ">=" (greater than or equal to), "<=" (less than or equal to), <> (not equal to).

Composite Key
A primary key consisting of two or more fields combined in such a way as to make a unique identifier.

Data Manipulation Language (DML)
A subset of SQL keywords that are used to add, remove, and modify data in a database. Examples include INSERT, UPDATE, and DELETE.

Data
Information that can be recorded and stored in a database.

Data Type
An attribute of a field that specifies what type of data that field can hold. Examples include numerical and text.

Database
A collection of data arranged for ease and speed of search and retrieval by a computer.

Database Administrator
A database professional responsible for the maintenance, security, and integrity of a database. Duties may include deciding who has access to what parts of the database and determining who can edit the database.

DB Browser
An SQL browser that uses the SQLite RDBMS.

Entity Relationship Diagram (ERD)
The graphical "blueprint" of a database that explains relationships between tables, such as a relationship between a primary key in one table and its corresponding foreign key(s) in other tables. An ERD can also be called a schema.

Field
A space allocated for a particular type of data. Field could refer to one specific item in a record or the entire column. Sometimes referred to as a column or attribute.

Foreign Key
A column in a table that is a primary key in another table.

Function
A special SQL keyword that accepts certain parameters called arguments, performs an operation (such as a calculation or modification of the data in the field), and returns the result of that operation as a value.

Integer
A data type that represents a whole (non-decimal) number.

Keyword
A special reserved word in SQL that performs a specific function in a statement or query. SELECT is the most common SQL keyword.

Logical Operator
An SQL keyword used to perform conditional selection of data meeting certain criteria, usually within a WHERE clause. Examples include BETWEEN, IN, LIKE, AND, and OR.

Messages Pane
A part of the SQL browser that gives the user feedback on the results of executed queries.

Metadata
Data about the structure of the data in a database.

Normalization
A technique used in the creation of databases to reduce redundant columns and thus decrease both the size of the database and the time required to run queries.

Operator
A special SQL keyword, usually used in conjunction with an existing SQL clause such as the WHERE clause. Common operators include comparison operators, logical operators, and arithmetic operators.

Primary Key
The column that acts as a unique identifier for a particular record in a table.

Query
A request made in Structured Query Language, entered into an SQL browser, requesting a specific set of information.

Query Pane
A part of the SQL browser that allows the user to enter SQL queries.

RDBMS
An abbreviation for relational database management system.

Record
One complete set of information, usually consisting of one row and at least one column.

Relational Database
A database design that employs multiple tables linked to each other by the use of primary and foreign key fields.

Relational Database Management System
A software package that allows the user to create, edit, and run SQL queries on relational databases.

Results Pane
The part of the SQL browser that shows the result set, or data returned from a query.

Result Set
The output or resulting data of a successfully executed query, usually in the form of records from the database.

Row
Another representation of a record.

Sandbox
A database environment that is isolated from any live servers or sensitive data so that code can be tested or practiced.

Schema
A description of the relationship between database tables and their primary and foreign keys that can be shown visually by an entity relationship diagram (ERD).

SQL
Structured Query Language. A standardized set of keywords specifically designed to create, manipulate, and control relational databases.

SQLite
A particular implementation of SQL, also called a relational database management system.

SQL Browser
The software interface of a relational database management system that allows an end user to browse databases and execute queries using Structured Query Language.

Statement
Any valid piece of code that can be executed by the RDBMS.

String
Text data stored in a text-based data type such as NVARCHAR.

Syntax
The correct keyword usage, order, and structure of SQL statements so that the SQL browser correctly interprets the resulting query.

Syntax Error
An error message created by the SQL browser due to an improperly structured query.

Table
A unique set of records, consisting of both rows and columns.

References

INTRODUCTION:

1.   "1 Second," Internet Live Stats, accessed January 24, 2019, http://www.internetlivestats.com/one-second/.

2.   https://www.forbes.com/sites/bernardmarr/2015/09/30/big-data-20-mind-boggling-facts-everyone-must-read/#36eb197c17b1.

3.   http://wikibon.org/blog/big-data-infographics/.

4.   https://www.dezyre.com/article/big-data-timeline-series-of-big-data-evolution/160.

5.   https://www.technologyreview.com/s/514346/the-data-made-me-do-it/.

6.   https://www.glassdoor.com/Salaries/sql-developer-salary-SRCH_KO0,13.htm.

CHAPTER 1:

7.   http://www.dictionary.com/browse/datum.

8.   https://www.seas.upenn.edu/~zives/03f/cis550/codd.pdf.

9.   "Most Widely Deployed SQL Database Engine - SQLite," accessed February 19, 2019, https://www.sqlite.org/mostdeployed.html.

CHAPTER 7:

10.   "SQLite Query Language: Core Functions," accessed February 25, 2019, https://www.sqlite.org/lang_corefunc.html

11.   "SQLite Query Language: Aggregate Functions," accessed March 10, 2019, https://www.sqlite.org/lang_aggfunc.html.

Index

Time and date data, 25–26, 26*f*
Timestring, 127, 127*f*–128*f*
Truncating text, 122–125
Tuple, 15
Two-pipe operator, 117*f*, 120–122
Type field, 42

U
Underscore symbol, 158
Unicode characters, 126
UPDATE statement, 168, 171–172
UPPER () function, 118, 125*f*, 126

V
Viewing individual records, 42–43, 42*f*
Views, 157–165, 179
   creating from joins, 160–163
   modifying, 160
   naming, 158, 160
   removing, 163–164
   subqueries and, 159–160

W
WHEN keyword, 85
WHERE clause, 67–69, 73–74, 109–110
   CASE statement and, 87–89
   dates used with, 78
   DELETE statement with, 172–173
   grouped queries with, 135–138
   HAVING clause *versus*, 138–139
   order of operations and, 81
   subqueries and, 146, 147*f*, 149–150
   UPDATE statement with, 171–172
Wildcards, 74–77, 75*f*–77*f*

Y
YouTube, 1

Notes

DOWNLOAD YOUR FREE CLYDEBANK MEDIA AUDIOBOOK FROM audible

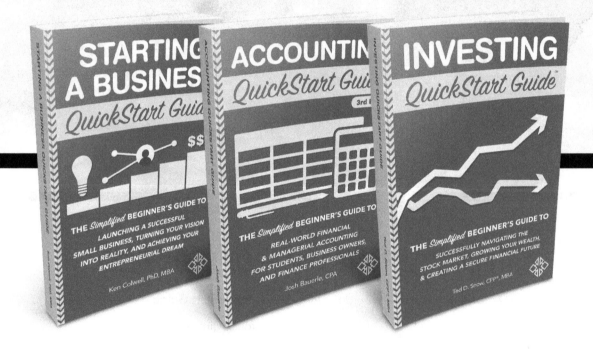

AdoptAClassroom.org

CPSIA information can be obtained
at www.ICGtesting.com
Printed in the USA
BVHW010811270320
576163BV00006B/86